D0848438

KEEPSAKES FOR THE HEART

KEEPSAKES FOR THE HEART

Becky Smith-Greer

PUBLISHING

Pomona, California

KEEPSAKES FOR THE HEART

Copyright © 1990 by Focus on the Family

Library of Congress Cataloging-in-Publication Data

Smith-Greer, Becky, 1943-
  Keepsakes for the heart : a tender story of sorrow and comfort / Becky Smith-Greer.
    p.   cm.
  ISBN 0-929608-98-4 : $12.99
  1. Smith-Greer, Becky, 1943-   2. Christian biography—United States.   3. Smith, Sonny, d. 1977.
4. Smith, Greg, d. 1977.   5. Bereavement—Religious aspects—Christianity.   6. Consolation.
I. Title.
BR1725.S59A3   1990
248.8'6'092—dc20
[B]   90-43629
                                                                                          CIP

Published by Focus on the Family Publishing, Pomona, CA 91799.

Distributed by Word Books, Dallas, Texas.

Scripture quotations are from:
The *Holy Bible: The New Scofield Reference Bible Authorized King James Version (KJV)*. Copyright ©
1909, 1917, 1937, 1945, 1967 by Oxford University Press, Inc.
The Living Bible (TLB). Copyright 1971 by Tyndale House Publishers.

Some people's names mentioned in this book have been changed to protect the privacy of the people
involved.

All rights reserved. No part of this publication may be reproduced, stored in a retrieval system, or transmit-
ted in any form or by any means—electronic, mechanical, photocopy, recording, or otherwise—without
prior permission of the copyright owner.

Edited by Sheila Cragg
Designed by Sherry Nicolai Russell
Cover photo by Ron Smith

Printed in the United States of America

90 91 92 93 94 95/10 9 8 7 6 5 4 3 2 1

To Tonya Smith, who is the daughter every mother dreams of and the joy of my life.

Max Lee Greer, who gives me strength, whose security in our love has allowed me to write this book, and whose prayers have sustained me day by day in the writing process. He is truly a gift from God, and I love him with all my heart.

Fred and Pauline Ballard, who gave me birth, roots and values.

Floyd and Barcie Smith, who made me their daughter and taught me the meaning of unselfish love.

Contents

Contents

Acknowledgments

I would like to express my deep gratitude to the following
people who helped make this book possible:

Harold Morris, my forever friend, whose deep faith and
unwavering love have provided a safe shelter for Tonya and me.
Without him, *Keepsakes for the Heart* would be a story untold.

S. Rickly Christian, who believed there was a story to share and
convinced me I had the ability to write it. His creativity,
encouragement, guidance and friendship gave me the confidence
I needed to try.

Sheila Cragg, gifted book editor from Focus on the Family
Publishing, who held my hand and coached me through the
"birthing" process. Today we share the joy of "motherhood."

Louise "Dixie" Pritcher and Laurinda Allison, whose unfailing
love and support kept me going every day as I tried to write in the
wee hours of the morning and maintain my responsibilities at
work.

CHAPTER ONE

Images for the Heart

THE *country road snaking up the mountain stretched dark and lonely before us. Gray clouds partially shadowed the moon* overhead. Our Volkswagen crept steadily upward, straining against the blasting winter wind. A flurry of snowflakes danced in the beam of our headlights.

"It's snowing. It's snowing," sang Tonya, our eight-year-old daughter, from the back seat of the car. "Look, Daddy," she exclaimed, wrapping her arms around his neck.

"Hot diggity dog," cheered Greg, our lanky twelve-year-old, leaning over my shoulder. "Now we can really have some fun."

In the dim dashboard light, I could see their shining hazel eyes and felt gratitude well up inside me. They were bright, healthy children, full of curiosity and excitement.

I glanced at my husband, Sonny. He was excited, too. I couldn't help smiling. A fresh snowfall could bring out the little boy in him even at thirty-five. A deep sense of contentment settled over me. Thirteen-and-a-half years of marriage had slipped by quickly, and everything was good for us right now. We were so happy.

"I hope it snows six inches, don't you?" Tonya said, patting her daddy's cheek.

"Not till after the program," he laughed. "We don't want to get snowed in at church, do we?"

Just then, we rounded the last curve leading to the mountaintop, and Mount Olivet Baptist Church came into view. Glowing warmly, it beckoned us home. My heart began to pound. Home for Christmas. Coming home to celebrate the sights and sounds of my childhood.

Instinctively, my eyes were drawn to the graveyard on the hillside to the left of the church. In the filtered moonlight, I could see the granite tombstones and bouquets of plastic flowers marking the graves of my grandparents and infant brother Clermon. Swirling snowflakes and dried leaves skipped across the graves before disappearing over the side of the mountain. A shiver inched up my spine.

The graveyard had always been a scary place to me, especially at night. Yet Sonny and I both knew this would someday be our final resting place. He had often told me that he wanted to lie here on this mountaintop forever with me by his side. Idle talk. Casual conversation made as we drove by the graveyard on our way to Daddy and Mama's house.

Yet I knew he really did love this western North Carolina mountain. He dreamed of building an A-frame cabin near the waterfalls on the land Daddy had given us. He teasingly called it "Ballard's Mountain" because so many of my aunts, uncles and cousins still lived here. He even appointed Mama "Mayor Pauline."

As soon as the car stopped, Tonya hopped out and darted for the church. Tonight, for the annual Christmas pageant, she was posing as an auburn-haired angel.

"I have to get my wings pinned on," she called, running toward the church.

"Hey, wait for me," yelled Greg, racing after her as he clutched his "rhinestone" crown atop his wavy auburn hair. He was a wise man. Sonny squeezed my hand as we hurried up the walk behind them.

Inside the church, the atmosphere was charged with excitement. Nervous chatter and stifled giggles sparked like electricity through the air. Little feet scurried underneath a curtain strung on a wire across the front. Greg and Tonya quickly disappeared behind it.

"Sh, sh, sh," the directors cautioned above the din.

As Sonny and I found a seat, I spied Mama and Daddy in the second row. Glancing around, I recognized most of the proud parents, grandparents and even aging great-grandparents squeezed into every wooden pew. Some men wore suits; others had on faded overalls. These were the people I loved. This was my heritage.

Soon the pianist began softly playing "Silent Night." The audience quieted as the lights dimmed. Out of the corner of my eye, I watched Sonny. A grin tugged at the side of his mouth, accenting the Kirk Douglas dimple on his chin. Thick, bushy eyebrows framed his slanted hazel eyes, making them almost disappear when he smiled. He had a glint in his eye, and I wondered what he was thinking—something zany, no doubt. His off-beat humor was the quality I treasured most about him.

Over his left ear, the tip of a horseshoe-shaped scar peeked from beneath his mass of wavy, auburn hair. Daisy, his horse, had stepped on his head when he was a boy growing up on a farm in Florida, the youngest of six children. I brushed some hair over the scar. Sonny smiled and slid his arm around me, resting it on the back of the pew.

3

I had grown up on a farm, too, about three miles away. The horse I had ridden was a one-eyed nag called Cricket. Every spring Daddy hitched her to a wooden plow and dug furrows across the open fields, where my whole family helped plant crops of beans, corn and other garden vegetables. To make ends meet for his family of seven, Daddy also worked the evening shift at the local cotton mill.

If we had any free time, my oldest sister Jerlene and I scurried into the woods to our playhouse. By tying strings around tree trunks, we made rooms filled with broken dishes, and crates and boxes for furniture. It was our castle in the woods. I became Princess Rose, ruler of the birds and baby dolls.

When I grew older, my interest turned naturally to boys. A cousin, Lula Mae, and I changed our names to Helen and Ellen. We created imaginary boyfriends, Bill and Bob. We dreamed of being beautiful brides, happy wives and proud mothers.

Sonny was my grown-up Bob, everything I had dreamed of and more. He was a loving husband, a wonderful father and my best friend. I was proud to be his wife.

Sonny and I met and married while we were students at Berry College in Rome, Georgia. After graduating we returned to my hometown, Hendersonville, North Carolina, to put down roots and raise our family. For ten years Sonny had been the band director at East Henderson High School.

Until Greg and Tonya were both in school, I had been a stay-at-home mom. Just the year before, I had returned to the classroom and was currently teaching kindergarten at Dana Elementary School.

Now, as we watched the Christmas story unfold through our children, I realized once again just how satisfying life had become for us. We had much to be thankful for.

After the pageant the families of my brother, Garland, and my sisters,

Jerlene, Dorothy and Margaret, gathered at Daddy and Mama's house for a Christmas Eve celebration that lasted far into the night.

Christmas morning dawned too early. It seemed like Sonny and I had hardly closed our eyes before Greg and Tonya were pouncing on us.

"Hurry up, you two," Greg said. "Get up. We can't wait any longer!"

"Go away!" Sonny groaned.

"Wake up now so we can look under the tree," Tonya pleaded, patting his face and pulling his eyes open.

We forced ourselves awake and hurried to the living room.

"Wow!" Greg shouted, as he opened a package and discovered his first grown-up watch.

'Oh, goodie. Barbie's camper," Tonya bubbled.

Before long the living room was strewn with gift paper, boxes and toys. After the excitement subsided, Sonny and Greg cooked a pancake breakfast while Tonya and I settled down to play with Barbie's new camper. After breakfast, we watched Greg's magic show. Since it was Sunday as well as Christmas, we began to get ready for church.

Greg was the first one dressed. Strutting around in his new forest green, three-piece suit, he thrust his thumbs in the watch pocket of his vest, stuck out his chest, then made faces at himself in the mirror. His 100-watt, rabbit-tooth grin made the freckles on the bridge of his nose stand out like copper pennies.

"Hurry up. It's time to go," he urged repeatedly, consulting his new watch.

"We've got to take some pictures first," Sonny said, putting film in the camera. "You two monkeys get ready."

Arms around each other, Greg and Tonya posed for keepsake portraits. Their infectious grins seemed to say, *Look at us. We're cute.*

Like the flicker of the camera shutter, I, too, was storing images, keepsakes for my heart. Only then, I did not know they would have to last a lifetime.

After church we ate lunch with Mama and Daddy and spent the afternoon enjoying the children and Christmas toys. We returned home late and prepared for our trip to see Granddaddy and Grandmother Smith in Florida the following day. Greg and Tonya hopped in bed as soon as their luggage was packed. Sonny and I took down the Christmas tree and straightened the house.

It was almost midnight before we finally climbed into bed. Cradled in the warmth and safety of Sonny's arms, I fell quickly asleep. Cuddling with him was the best part of any day for me.

We got up at five the next morning, and by the time I had dressed, Sonny, Greg and Tonya had packed our Volkswagen and were raring to go. "Anything else?" Sonny asked, turning off the house lights, locking the door and joining us in the car.

Just as Sonny started the ignition, Greg suddenly jumped up and shouted frantically, "Wait a minute, Daddy, we're about to forget the most important thing!"

"What is it, son?"

"Just let me have the house keys. I can get 'em real quick," he said.

We waited while Greg disappeared into the house. In a minute he was back, grinning from ear to ear. He held up two fishing rods and a tackle box. "Daddy, we were about to leave our fishin' stuff," he said sheepishly. "Don't you think Uncle Jack and Richard will want to go fishin' with us at Orange Lake?"

As we pulled out of the driveway, the car headlights pierced the hovering fog shrouding our red brick home. It was our first home, and it seemed so secure and solid, silhouetted in the blackness.

We made frequent rest stops, played Password and sang as we traveled down through Georgia into Florida. Late that afternoon, the anticipated Alachua exit came into view. Bouncing in the back seat, Tonya exclaimed, "Just think, Greg, Grandma's acre peas and pumpkin pie. I can't wait!"

As we passed Santa Fe High School, Sonny's alma mater, Greg asked innocently, "Daddy, did you have a girlfriend before you met Mama?"

"Have a girlfriend?" asked Sonny, raising his eyebrows and shrugging his shoulders. "Son, I had so many girlfriends, I put 'em all in the back of Granddaddy's truck and give 'em a number. I'd bring 'em up front one at a time just for the privilege of riding beside me."

"Ah, Daddy, you did not."

"Sure I did," teased Sonny. "When you're ready, I'll let you borrow my truck so you can, too. The girls will line up just to ride with you."

It tickled me to watch the changes in Greg now that he was in junior high school. He had finally mustered the courage to ask his first girl to a sock hop and restyled his hair for the occasion. Recently his voice had begun to change, and I had caught him examining his chin, looking for signs of fuzz. I wondered if Granddaddy and Grandmother would notice the changes in Greg.

As soon as we pulled into the yard and the car stopped, Greg and Tonya jumped out and ran for the house. The door opened and Granddaddy Smith appeared. The children ran straight into his open arms and hugged him. Granddaddy was seventy-seven years old. His shoulders were stooped and rounded from a life of hard work on the farm. Over the years, his steps had become slower, and the glasses a little thicker, but two things about him never changed—his crew cut and open arms.

As we hugged on the steps, I spied Grandmother in the kitchen. She was peeking in the oven. Her stylish blue dress was crisp and clean; her short silver hair was brushed away from her face. I could tell by the way she nodded her head that the turkey and dressing were baking right on schedule. The aroma of spices and turkey greeted us as we joined her in the kitchen.

7

"Welcome home," she said. After hugging each one of us, she wiped steam from her glasses. Cooking was Grandmother's special way of loving. She was the only woman I knew who had two stoves in her kitchen.

The house was already brimming with family members. Greeting cards decorated the den table, a red poinsettia sat atop the TV, and Christmas presents were piled under the tree. Tonya and Greg immediately checked the refrigerator for pumpkin pies. Satisfied, they ran to find eight-month-old baby Amber, the newest great-grandchild.

After a delectable Christmas feast, we gathered around the tree to open presents and share family news. We rejoiced with our nephew Richard, who had started his first job as a pharmacist. He had recently graduated with honors from Southwestern Oklahoma State University. Our niece Cheryl flashed a diamond and proudly introduced Skip, her future husband. He soon found out that teasing was the official sign of acceptance into the Smith family. The laughter and banter went on late into the night.

As eyelids grew heavy and yawns began to punctuate the conversation, the families began to depart. We hugged Sonny's older brother Fred; his wife, Martha; and son, Ronnie, as they left for their home in Georgia. Sonny's oldest sister Kat and her husband, Howard, lived only a couple of miles away, so we would see more of them during our visit. Another sister Floy; her husband, Jack; and their son, Richard, had flown from Arlington, Texas, in their new, single-engine airplane. They were spending the night with Jack's mother in nearby High Springs.

We said our goodbyes in the dim porch light with promises of seeing each other the next day. When the last car drove out of sight, Granddaddy and Grandmother Smith turned back into the house.

"We'll be there in a minute," Sonny said, putting his arm around me and pulling me close.

In silence, we walked past Granddaddy's workshop toward the pasture fence in back of the house. Above us, the stars twinkled, and the moon played peek-a-boo with a cluster of clouds. The house and barn of the nearby dairy farm were silhouetted in the darkness. The cattle were asleep. The only sounds were our footsteps softly crunching the dried grass and silky sand. The barren fields stretched before us as far as the eye could see. The world was at peace.

We reached the fence and stopped. Sonny was silent. Intuitively I felt he was remembering his times as a boy when he plowed the fields, hunted dove, rode old Daisy across the meadows or romped with Rex, his dog, in the watermelon patch.

Down the road to our left stood a darkened frame house. Mrs. Hines lived there, alone now. Her husband had died. *Christmas must be so lonely for her,* I thought, snuggling closer to Sonny.

Behind her house, a solitary cluster of trees were framed by the black sky. They seemed like a symbol of life in the barrenness of winter. I shivered as a faint rustle of leaves stirred above us in the breeze. Darkness surrounded us when the house lights went out. Grandmother and Granddaddy had gone to bed. The long day was over for them. Another Christmas had passed.

"I love you, Beck," Sonny whispered, nuzzling his chin in my hair.

"I love you, too, sweetheart," I murmured, kissing his neck.

Slowly we turned toward the house. How could I know that tonight, for the last time, I would sleep in my precious husband's arms?

CHAPTER TWO

There's Been an Accident

THE *next morning after breakfast, Granddaddy, Grandmother, Sonny and I lingered over coffee and basked in the sunshine* pouring through the kitchen window. The sun seemed to give the day a happy beginning.

Greg and Tonya scampered outside and soon disappeared into Granddaddy's workshop. In a while, they reappeared and raced for the lattice swing hanging from the oak tree. I watched them through the open window above the sink.

"Push me first, Greg," Tonya demanded, jumping in the swing. Patiently he pushed. Whatever she wanted, he usually did. From the moment he first held her on the way home from the hospital, he had loved her protectively. He had cradled her, rubbed her bald head and tried to make her laugh.

Sonny felt the same about Tonya. Once I had asked him, "If you could isolate the single happiest moment in your life, what would it be?"

Without hesitating, he replied, "The moment Tonya was born."

"Why would you say that?"

"Well, I have a job I love, a wonderful wife, a fine son and finally a beautiful daughter. What more could a man want out of life?"

We were still sitting in the kitchen when we heard the whine of a car engine. Greg and Tonya gave a shout and ran to greet Jack, Floy and Richard. We met them at the door.

"Uncle Jack, did you really buy that plane yourself?" Greg wanted to know immediately.

"Yeah, we did, little buddy," Jack answered, bending down to give him a hug. "We wanted to fly to Granddaddy and Grandmother Smith's to see you."

Jack was about six-foot, and at forty-nine, he was beginning to bald. The brown hair circling the bottom half of his head was peppered with gray like his stubby mustache. He was lean, trim and distinguished-looking. Jack was a gentle man and loved children. For twenty-five years, he had been a Scout master with the Boy Scouts. It was an interest he shared with his son, Richard. Both were Eagle Scouts.

"Aunt Floy," Tonya interrupted, "what's the nickname Daddy calls you sometimes? I forgot."

"Honey Bunch," replied Jack.

Tonya giggled, "No, silly."

"You mean Mutsy?" asked Sonny.

"Yeah, Little Mutsy?" Tonya said with a laugh. "They named you that 'cause you're so tiny."

"Tonya, you know something funny about Aunt Floy's name?" Greg asked with a grin. "She was a Smith and Uncle Jack is a Smith, so her name is Aunt Floy Smith-Smith. If you marry a Smith, then your name will be T-Bug Smith-Smith. Little T-Bug," he teased.

"Greg, stop that right now!"

"Ah, I'm only teasing. I love you, little T-Bug," Greg laughed, patting her head and fueling her fire. He turned to his uncle and said, "Uncle Jack, did you know when Tonya was born Daddy took me for an airplane ride over the hospital? That was fun.

"T-Bug, you were the cutest little baby. What happened to you?" Greg laughed as she chased him around the yard. Circling back to Richard, he asked, "Will you help me do experiments with my chemistry set?"

"Sure, little buddy. Let's go."

While they concocted vile-smelling mixtures, Tonya held the bottles. Jack, Floy, Grandmother, Granddaddy, Sonny and I sat in the kitchen, drank coffee and talked.

Seeing Jack's and Floy's devotion to each other was an inspiration to me. Even after twenty-seven years their marriage was strong. They had three children—Richard, twenty-six; Peggy, twenty-four; and Carol, twenty. Jack was an engineer with Bell Helicopter, and Floy was a branch manager with the Educational Employees Credit Union.

Later that morning the men decided the weather was perfect for taking an airplane ride over to the Florida coast. After lunch Greg was so excited he could hardly contain himself. He gobbled down a sandwich and began to pace, but no one was moving fast enough for him. Exasperated, he started striding through the house, fuming. I could always tell when he or his daddy were upset; they walked fast.

"Greg," Sonny said sternly, "come here, son."

Slowly Greg turned and shuffled back. Sonny whispered in his ear, and Greg sat down, a look of dejection on his face. Sonny's discipline was never harsh; it was always quiet and done in love.

Finally, about one-thirty, everyone was ready to leave. Normally Tonya wanted to be wherever her daddy and Greg were, but today she decided to go shopping with Floy, Grandmother and me. Tonya wanted to buy baby Amber a present with the five dollars she had received for Christmas. Granddaddy Smith did not feel like going anywhere, so he stayed home alone. We all agreed to meet back at the house by four.

Greg gave me a quick hug. "Bye, Mom, love you," he said, dashing to the car. He was the first one in.

"Mr. Smith, we're going to fly over the house to snap some pictures," Jack said. "When you hear the airplane, will you come outside so we can take your picture from the air?"

"Okay," agreed Granddaddy.

"Floy, you and Becky stand over by the sycamore tree and let me take your picture. Floy, put on your new coat," Jack said, opening the car door and taking out the camera and a black fur coat.

"Wow, let me feel that," I said, stroking the fur as he handed it to Floy. "That's the real thing, isn't it?"

Jack grinned, pleased I had noticed. It was his Christmas gift to Floy, her first mink coat.

"I'll never be able to afford a mink coat on a teacher's salary. Let me just stand near yours, okay?" I laughed. Wrapping herself in the fur, Floy giggled as she playfully modeled for Jack. She was a striking picture with her black hair, brown eyes and sparkling smile.

As we started to leave, Sonny grinned and said, "Bye, Babe, I love you." He hugged me close, and we kissed goodbye.

"I love you, too," I responded, clinging to him for an extra moment. "We'll be home about four."

I waved goodbye until they disappeared, then I got in the car with Grandmother, Floy and Tonya.

At the Gainesville Mall, we had fun jostling through the crowd of after-Christmas shoppers. We looked for bargains, sprayed ourselves with perfume and tried on diamond rings. Tonya stayed close to Floy, holding her hand and playing with her big gold ring. Soon it was time to start home.

Chatting gaily, I maneuvered Granddaddy's tan, compact Chevrolet through bumper-to-bumper Christmas traffic out of the city toward the beautiful countryside. As we neared the interchange of Interstate 75, I noticed the gas needle registering near empty and pulled into an Exxon station.

Before I had time to turn off the car ignition, the right back door was jerked open. I snapped around to see our niece Joan Rodriquez leaning inside. Her face was ashen, her blue eyes full of terror. She had been sent to intercept us, knowing we would be traveling this road home.

With controlled, determined quietness, she grimly uttered, "Listen, you all, there's been an accident in the airplane. We don't know how bad yet...."

As quickly as I could blink, fear ripped through my body. I began to shiver. *An accident in the airplane! Oh, God, no!*

Suddenly I wanted to run and hide, to flee from the conversation between Joan, Grandmother and Floy. I didn't want to hear. I didn't want to know.

Desperate to get away, I shoved open the car door and ran to the service station bathroom. Locking the door behind me, I fell back against it, afraid to breathe.

I closed my eyes and listened for footsteps. For the moment no one could make me hear what I did not want to hear. I struggled to stop trembling.

"Becky, calm down," I said aloud. "It's going to be all right. Get hold of yourself."

Over and over, Joan's words pounded in my head, growing louder and louder: "There's been an accident in the airplane! There's been an accident in the airplane!"

"Becky, don't think! Open your eyes," I commanded.

I opened my eyes wide and moved woodenly toward the mirror. Suddenly through gritted teeth, I screamed threateningly, "God, you can't do this to us!"

Paralyzed with fear, I stared in the mirror until a pounding on the door jarred me back to reality.

"Becky, are you all right?" Joan called urgently.

"Yes, I'll be out in a minute," I responded, hurrying into the rest-room stall. I sat down on the commode, and my stomach started to churn. Mud was smeared on the dirty gray floor beneath my feet. On the door, "Jane loves Ben" was scribbled inside a heart with an arrow. The flamingo-pink paint had begun to peel around the door hinges. I knew I needed to hurry, but I felt powerless to move; being locked in the bathroom stall was safer than being outside.

Eventually, I walked to the sagging turquoise sink to wash my hands. As I turned on the faucet, brown water gushed from the rusted pipes. I twisted the old-fashioned porcelain knob to full force and waited for the water to run clear. Splashing water on my face, I struggled to control the nausea sloshing around in my stomach.

I raised my head and glanced in the mirror. The young woman staring back at me seemed like a stranger. The hazel eyes with a dark blue outer rim looked like mine. The heart-shaped upper lip was the same. She had short, frosted-blonde hair. She was about my age, thirty-four, and looked like me.

I reached up and touched the faded mirror. For the first time, I noticed a wavy crack running from top to bottom. Part of me was on one side of the crack, part on the other. Inside I felt as if I were splitting in half, too.

"Becky, they're waiting on you," I said aloud. "You can't think about it now."

With steeled determination, I began to scoop up my emotions and stuff them into a tiny box hidden in the recesses of my heart. I would deal with my emotions later. I slammed the box shut, somehow knowing I was preparing for survival.

Hesitant and fearful, I finally opened the door and took a deep breath. Cars were still whizzing by on Interstate 75. People were still milling around the Exxon station. The sun was even shining. To everyone else, the whole world was still the same. To me, everything had changed.

Trying to shift the weight pressing in on me, I took a deep breath and squared my shoulders. Then, very slowly, I walked back to the car and an uncertain future.

CHAPTER THREE

A Family Cut in Half

ONLY *a few minutes had passed since I ran for safety in the service station rest room. It seemed an eternity.*

When I returned to the car, Joan said, "Becky, I'll drive you home. Paul will drive our car."

"Oh, no, I'll drive. I must drive," I pleaded. My heart pounded violently. I felt as if I might explode, if I did not have something to do with my hands.

"Okay," she reluctantly agreed. "We'll be right behind you."

"Honey, will you sit by me and help me watch the speedometer?" I asked Tonya, pulling her close. I needed to touch her; she was real. At that moment, my love for her was almost desperate.

"Mama, do you think they're in the hospital?"

"I don't know," I hedged. "I'm sure Daddy and Greg are all right. They probably had to make an emergency landing." Visions raced through my mind. I tried to blot out the thought that Greg and Sonny were dead. Gripping the steering wheel, I locked my arms and frantically tried to steady my trembling hands.

"If they're hurt, we'll have to be their nurses, won't we?" asked Tonya, patting me.

In the back seat, Floy and Grandmother Smith continued grappling with the shocking news we had just received. Their voices sounded distant and hollow.

"Maybe something minor went wrong with the plane," Grandmother suggested.

"I don't understand it," Floy said. "Jack and Richard are such careful pilots. I just pray they're not hurt."

Why won't they be quiet? I wondered. I felt as if I had been let in on a hellish secret they could not grasp. *All four of them—Jack, Richard, Sonny and Greg—are dead. I know it. They are dead! People don't survive a small airplane crash. It's all so plain and final. Why don't they understand? Why won't they be quiet?*

I did not want Tonya listening to their conversation, so I tried to keep her occupied with mindless chatter. Anxious thoughts, however, careened wildly through my head. *Where did the plane crash? Maybe they are not dead...their bodies are broken...are they suffering?...oh, God, no...not my Greg. He could never stand pain... blood scares him.... Stop it, Becky. Stop thinking like this,* I told myself over and over as we neared the Smiths' farm.

A few hundred yards before reaching the house, we passed Mrs. Hines's home on the left. Underneath a lone grove of trees, I spied a cluster of cars. Then suddenly, without warning, there it was—the downed plane.

Like a hot iron, the image seared my mind and heart forever. A crumpled mass of metal. An airplane wing jutting out of the ground.

An open field. I quickly looked away. I could not stand to see anymore. I did not want to feel. I did not want to know what I knew.

I eased the car into the yard, careful not to pull past the house toward the garage. Otherwise, I would have a direct view of the downed plane.

As I came to a stop, Sonny's oldest sister, Kat, rushed toward us. Her brown eyes were red and swollen, her face streaked with tears. Panic showed in her eyes. "Becky, where's Tonya?" she asked, her voice pleading.

"Tonya's with me," I answered, grabbing her little hand as she scooted out of the seat behind me.

Relief flooded Kat's face. "Oh, thank God," she cried, her voice cracking. "We thought she was in the plane, too. It's bad, Beck."

"No!" I screamed. "I don't want to hear anymore!"

Pushing past her, I turned to Paul, Joan's husband. "Paul, will you go see how bad it is? Please, see if they're hurt," I pleaded. Then pulling Tonya along with me, I ran toward the house.

I jerked open the door to find Granddaddy standing before me, pain and fear twisting his face. "Oh, Becky," he groaned.

Suddenly my legs buckled. I fell to the floor. Driven by fear, I jumped up. Still pulling Tonya, I ran to the bedroom. Slamming the door behind me, I pulled the shades and closed the curtains to shut out reality.

I sat on the bed and hugged Tonya close to me. "Honey, I don't know why they're trying to hurt us. Daddy and Greg aren't going to leave us," I said, stroking her hair. "They love us too much. We're too happy. I wish everyone could understand that. We just won't listen to them." I continued, rocking back and forth. "We'll stay in here away from everyone. Daddy and Greg will be home in a little while. We'll just wait here for them."

Before long, Tonya started to squirm. "Mama, I want to go outside and see the airplane."

"No! No, honey, you can't do that," I responded, tightening my grip on her. "You have to stay here with me." Rocking faster, I fingered the corkscrew curls at the nape of her neck. I had to protect her. I had to protect myself from what was going on outside.

After a while, Tonya started again. "Mama, please let me go and see Aunt Floy."

"No, honey, you can't do that."

"Then just let me go watch TV in the den."

"All right," I reluctantly agreed, "if you promise not to go outside."

"I won't," she said, hurrying out the bedroom door.

For hours, my desperate need to hide kept me closeted away in the bedroom. I refused to listen to, much less believe or see, what was happening outside the bedroom walls. I sat on the bed, hugged a pillow and continued rocking. It was December the twenty-seventh, only two days after Christmas, but Christmas seemed unreal to me; it seemed so long ago.

Throughout the late afternoon, Kat and her husband Howard, Floy, Grandmother, Granddaddy, family friends and the pastor from Forest Grove Baptist Church came into the bedroom and tried to talk to me. I simply refused to listen. Denial was survival. If I did not hear it, it would not be true.

On one of Kat's frequent trips to the bedroom, she asked, "Beck, can Joan take Tonya down to Carlton and Imogene's house to play with Amber? It would be better for her right now."

"Okay," I agreed.

Day turned to night. Sometimes I felt great pity, concern and deep love for Floy. Jack and Richard were dead. I wondered where she was, how she was doing. Had she called her daughters, Peggy and Carol? Where were they? How did they feel? At other times, I was overwhelmed for Granddaddy and Grandmother Smith. They had lost Sonny, their

22

baby boy; Jack, their son-in-law of twenty-seven years; and two grandsons, Richard and Greg. I loved Granddaddy and Grandmother so much my heart ached. But I was trying so desperately to hold back the emotional hell threatening to erupt inside me that I couldn't dwell on what was taking place outside the bedroom walls. I fluctuated in and out of reality—acknowledging what I knew one moment, refusing it the next.

About nine that evening, Howard came into the bedroom again. His usual smile was now a grimace; pain was deeply evident in his blue eyes. I knew Howard would be honest with me.

Hesitantly I asked him, "Howard, are they. . . ." I couldn't bring myself to say that final, ugly word.

He took both my hands and looked directly into my eyes, "Yes, honey, they are. . . ."

"No! No! No!" I screamed. Jerking free from his grip, I covered my ears. "I don't want to hear it!"

"Becky," Kat said, joining us, "we need to know what funeral home to send them to. You've got to talk to us now."

"No, I don't," I cried, shaking my head furiously. I arose from the bed and paced the room. My hands trembled as I tore at my hair. "You only send dead bodies to funeral homes. Sonny and Greg aren't dead, and I wish you would stop saying that!"

"I guess we'll just have to do what we think best," Kat said quietly, as she and Howard left the room. I grabbed a pillow and clutched it against my stomach. I felt as if an invisible person was hurling poison darts at me, trying to kill me. I would not survive, if they did not leave me alone.

Sometimes I was aware of the time, other times not. I was rocking back and forth when a strangely familiar voice called my name. Then I felt two strong arms grab me in a bear hug. It was Roscoe Green, Sonny's best friend. They were like brothers. "I'm here, Becky," he said, his voice choking with emotion.

For an instant, I collapsed in the safety of his arms. "Oh, Roscoe," I pleaded, "make this nightmare go away."

"I wish I could, Becky. I wish I could," he whispered.

"Honey, is there anything we can do for you?" asked Peggy, Roscoe's wife, encircling us both in an embrace.

"I don't think so, just stay with me for a while."

Before long, Tonya burst into the room. "I'm home, Mama," she announced. "I love that Amber. She's the cutest little thing. I had so much fun playing with her."

Seeing Peggy and Roscoe, Tonya bubbled, "Where are Lauralee and Julianne? Can they play with me?"

"They're not with us this time," Peggy replied. "Maybe you can go home with us."

"I don't think so," I answered. "I need her close to me."

"I'm going to see who's in the den," Tonya said, bouncing out of the room.

"I don't think she understands what happened, do you?" I questioned.

"I wish she didn't have to," Roscoe said sadly.

A steady stream of people continued to come in and out of the bedroom while Peggy and Roscoe were with me. When everyone finally left, I got up and walked to the window. Desperately, I wanted to pull back the curtain and open the shade, but fear kept me paralyzed.

Later, Kat and Howard came back and confronted me again. "You've got to call your parents, Becky," Kat insisted. "The news of the crash has already gone to the press, and it will be on the eleven o'clock TV news in Hendersonville. You don't want your parents to hear it that way, do you?"

"No, I guess not."

"Then go call them now."

24

Fearfully I opened the door and tiptoed to the phone in the hall. My fingers trembled when I tried to find the holes in the old-fashioned black dial. Something inside stopped me. Daddy and Mama loved Sonny and Greg as much as if they were their own. How could I tell them they were dead? They were at home alone and might not be able to handle the news. I had better have someone else go tell them. I thought of my younger sister Dottie. Her husband, Ted, was strong. He would be able to go tell Mama and Daddy.

"Operator, person to person to Ted Beddingfield, please," I said. Dottie answered the phone.

"He's not here," I heard her say. "Is there a message?" "No, operator. No message. Thank you," I whispered, trying to disguise my voice. Dottie was alone. I could not tell her.

Jerlene. Call Jerlene, I thought. *She's strong. She will go.*

"Hello," she said.

"Jerl, this is Beck. I need you to do something for me." I said quietly, trying not to choke up. "Sonny and Greg went for an airplane ride with Jack and Richard this afternoon. The plane crashed. Sonny and Greg are dead."

"No, Beck, no!" she cried, stunned. "Are you sure?"

"They're gone; they're all gone!" I began to weep. "Jack and Richard, too. Will you go tell Mama and Daddy for me? They'll need someone with them when they hear it."

"Of course, I will," she said. Only the sound of our sobs echoed over the telephone wires.

As I hung up the phone, my thoughts turned to Sonny's band kids. What would they do? How would they be able to handle the news? For the past ten years, Sonny had poured his life into building the band program at East High. In that time, hundreds of students had become part of our lives. They started beginner band in seventh grade and usually stayed with us until their high school graduation. We loved each one as though they were our own. What would happen to them now?

"Oh, God, please!" I cried aloud. "Won't somebody tell me this is not happening? Won't somebody wake me up from this nightmare! It can't be real!"

Suddenly I became aware that I was thirsty. Wandering to the kitchen for a glass of water, I found the house teeming with people—newspaper reporters, friends bringing food, friends offering help, and friends who just needed to cry with us.

I felt panic rising in me. Quickly I turned and escaped back to the bedroom. Tonya was now sleeping peacefully in the middle of the bed. About two o'clock in the morning, when the noise finally settled, I crept down the hall to the kitchen. Grandmother, Floy and Kat were sitting silently around the kitchen table. Without a word, I joined them. Only the ticking of the clock echoed in the stillness as grief bonded our souls.

A telephone ring broke the silence. Kat answered it in the hall. "Becky, it's for you," she said.

It was Dr. Dean Weaver, my pastor, from North Carolina. He and his wife, Jeanitha, had been vacationing with their son in south Georgia when they heard the news of the crash. They had driven down to Florida to be with Tonya and me. "Becky, we're here in High Springs. Could you give me directions to the house?" he asked.

In a few minutes, I heard the car pull into the yard and met them at the door. Dr. Weaver had been my pastor for six years. He had baptized Greg and Tonya. Sonny had worked under him with the youth and music programs of our church. Their daughter, Dale, had been one of Sonny's chorus students and their son, John, was a band member. Our roots and love for each other were deep. Tonight I was especially grateful for their presence. They brought a touch of home.

Before long, Sonny's oldest brother, Paul, and his wife, Faye, arrived from Tennessee. We visited briefly, but everyone was weary from the long day, and so they left to get some rest. Grandmother and Floy decided to lie down, too. For the rest of the night, I sat alone, huddled in the den beside the gas heater, trying not to think or feel. As I gazed at the flickering flames, I fingered the quilting on my new light green housecoat. Sonny had given it to me for Christmas. I was grateful for it; it was warm.

As morning broke across the sky, I wandered into the bedroom where Sonny and I had cuddled just a few hours before. Tonya was still asleep. Tenderly, I touched her sweet little face and gently brushed back her hair, trying not to wake her. She was so much like her daddy with her auburn hair and fun-loving personality.

What a happy family we had been. Our pleasures were simple— camping, walking in the woods, riding through the mountains in our old green Chevy truck. I could still picture Tonya as a toddler, standing beside her daddy, her arm around his neck, patting his cheek or squeezing his lips to make him talk like Donald Duck.

How could I tell her that her daddy was dead? That he would never again tuck her into bed? That he would never again give her a goodnight kiss or tell her how much he loved her?

How could I tell her that the brother she loved was gone? She would never again be his assistant in magic shows or go fishing with him. She would never again ride her bike with him to Peace's Grocery for ice cream or play in the creek with him and Fonzie, our black poodle.

How could I tell my baby girl our family had been cut in half?

CHAPTER FOUR

Invisible Wounds

SOON *after daybreak, friends began bringing breakfast. Movement was quiet, talking hushed. Tonya awoke about* eight and got dressed. "Where's Daddy and Greg, Mama? Didn't they come home last night?" she asked innocently.

"No, honey, but maybe they'll be here before too long," I said. "Why don't you go eat some breakfast?"

"Mama, they're really dead. Everybody says they're dead but you."

"Scoot, scoot, scoot. Get some breakfast now. You want to be ready when Joan brings Amber, don't you?" I said.

After Tonya left, I started to tidy the room and make the bed. The memory of waking up in Sonny's arms the morning before was still fresh in my mind. Grandmother Smith joined me, and without speaking she grasped a corner of the sheet and started to tuck it in.

When our eyes met, I whispered, "Mom, may I have these sheets?"

Tears silently trickled down our cheeks as she nodded yes. She understood.

Together we folded the yellow flowered sheets. As she handed them to me, I gently touched her aged hand in wordless thanks. She had already given me so much—her love, her son.

Before long Howard and Kat arrived. "Becky, funeral arrangements have to be made. You wouldn't talk to us last night, so we had them taken to Copeland's Funeral Home in Gainesville. You've got to come with us now and select the caskets," Kat lovingly commanded. Weariness lined her face.

Funeral home? Fear and panic knotted my stomach. "No! No! No!" I begged, shaking my head vigorously in disbelief. "I can't do that. Please don't make me do that." I backed away from Kat. "Won't you and Howard do it for me? Whatever you select will be fine. I just can't go."

Fear of death overwhelmed me. I was afraid of what I would find, of what I would see. *If I don't go, it won't be real,* I thought anxiously. As long as I could shut out reality, I could survive.

"Of course, we will, Beck," Kat assured me, wrapping me in her arms. "But you've got to decide where you want them buried."

Anxiously I searched Grandmother's lined, tear-stained face. Once again our eyes met.

"Becky, don't worry about us," she said. "It's your decision. Whatever you decide is fine with us."

With those words, Grandmother showed me the real meaning of unselfish love. She also affirmed my ability to decide what was right for my own family.

"I have to take them home," I said, as images of the graveyard beside the tiny mountain church flashed through my mind. "They've got to be at home on Ballard's Mountain."

"Beck, now I've got to have some clothes to take to the funeral home," Kat said. "Get me their clothes."

Anxious to have her gone before she insisted I go with her, I turned toward the closet. As I reached for Greg's green suit, a tidal wave of painful reality washed over me with such force, I staggered and fell against the door frame. My little son was dead! Never again would I touch his freckled face, see his rabbit-tooth grin or hear him call me, "Mama."

"Oh, my baby. My son," I sobbed, burying my face in his green suit. "Greg, oh my little Greg."

"Beck, you can't do this now," Kat whispered in my ear as she cradled me in her arms. "Honey, you've got to stay strong. We all do. There's too much facing us ahead. You can't break now," she said soothingly as if trying to convince herself, too.

I straightened. Gently she tugged at Greg's suit in my hand. Slowly my fingers uncurled and released it to her.

"Now we'll need something for Sonny," she said, wiping tears from her own eyes. I knew Kat felt my pain. She was sixteen when Sonny was born. She had taken care of him, changed his diapers, wiped his nose and rocked him to sleep. When he was a teenager, she bought him new clothes, loaned him her car and slipped him dating money. He was like her own child, instead of her baby brother.

"He didn't bring a suit, just his blue pants and plaid sport coat. Here is his white shirt and blue tie. They'll need clean underwear, too," I said, hurrying across the room to the old-fashioned brown chest of drawers.

Quickly rummaging through the drawers, I chose the newest, whitest pair of underwear and freshest T-shirts I could find for both of them. As I handed them to Kat, I could still smell the lingering fragrance of fabric softener. I felt a fleeting sense of satisfaction. They would both be clean and well-dressed. My two men were so handsome that way.

"Kat, can I ask one more favor?" I pleaded. "Will you get me Sonny's

31

wedding band? He's never had it off." It was a part of him I could keep.

"We'll take care of everything," she promised. "Are you sure you won't go with us?"

"Oh, no!" I said, feeling panicky again. "I can't. Please don't ask me. Just go. Please, just go."

"Okay, we will," Kat said, gathering up the clothes we had selected. "Joan said she is coming to get Tonya this morning and take her back to our house for the day."

Peeking from behind the shade, I watched Kat and Howard drive away and breathed a sigh of relief. Once again I closed the bedroom door and sat down in the middle of the empty, queen-size bed. Slowly I drew up my legs, wrapped my arms around them and rested my chin on my knees. I pulled the floral sheets Grandmother had just given me over my feet to keep them warm. Gently I began to rock. *Don't think, Becky, just don't think about it,* I told myself over and over.

In a short while, Tonya came to tell me my pastor and his wife had returned. I joined them at the kitchen table.

"Becky, the Lord has given me the most beautiful Scripture for the service," Dean began. "It's 2 Samuel 1:23. David says, 'Saul and Jonathan *were* lovely and pleasant in their lives, and in their death they were not divided (KJV).' Sonny and Greg were certainly pleasant in their lives, and in death they were not divided. Do you like that?"

"Yes, it's so beautiful and appropriate, isn't it?" I said, as we all fought to control our tears.

"Have you thought about the funeral? We really must talk about it now," Dr. Weaver urged. "Are you going to have the service here or at home?"

"At home. Shepherd's Funeral Home will be in charge."

"What about ministers?" Dean continued, pressing me forward as he was making notes.

"You'll do it, won't you? I'd also like to use Reverend Eugene Johnston and Reverend Harold McKinnish."

"You'll need to call them right away," he said. "What about visitation?"

"Oh, no, I don't want that!" I spewed so vehemently I even surprised myself. "I detest that custom. I don't want people filing by the caskets to look at them."

"Becky, of course, you don't have to if you don't want to," Dr. Weaver said. "But people need to let you know how much they love you and how deeply they grieve for Sonny and Greg. If you can force yourself to go through that time and give them an opportunity to express their love, it will save you a lot of anguish later."

"I'll think about it," I replied, still not convinced.

By the time we finished making arrangements for the service, the house was starting to fill up with people again. I wandered aimlessly, unaware of who was even there. Somehow I knew Floy was in High Springs taking care of Jack's mother and making funeral arrangements. Her daughters, Peggy and Carol, were due to arrive from Texas.

I was also aware that Granddaddy and Grandmother Smith were distraught with grief. Everyone was greatly concerned for their well-being. At their age, the shock and loss were almost too much for them to bear. Sonny's brothers, Fred and Paul, were taking care of them. I wanted to help but felt detached and powerless. It seemed as if I were viewing what was happening around me like it was a slow-motion movie. Nothing seemed real.

About two o'clock that afternoon, Kat and Howard returned from the funeral home. We retreated to the bedroom.

"Beck, we hope you will like the caskets we chose," Kat said. "We tried to get them as much alike as possible. They're both silver gray. Not too ornate. Masculine-looking. I think you'll be pleased."

"Oh, Kat, I know I will. Thank you for doing this for me," I said, clinging to her.

"Howard, did you see Sonny and Greg?"

"Yes, honey, we did."

"How are they?" I asked, inwardly bracing myself for the answer. I was terrified to hear his response. I felt as if I were waiting for someone to stab me in the heart with a knife. I closed my eyes and held my breath, waiting.

"Becky, they're fine," he said quietly.

"You mean they're not broken? They're whole?" I could not believe what he was saying.

"No, they're not broken. They're both badly bruised and swollen, but their faces and bodies are not cut and torn."

"Oh, thank God," I whispered, tears trickling down my cheeks.

"I think it would be best for you not to see them, though," Howard continued. "Just remember them the way they were when they left you."
He did not have to persuade me. I was too afraid to see them. I did not know if he were telling me the truth or only telling me what he felt I could handle. I chose to believe they were whole because I wanted to believe it. I needed to believe it. If I did not see them, I would never really know. I could remember them as they were—happy, vibrant, full of life and laughter.

Another question burned inside me. I had to know. Dealing with this nightmare one small piece at a time was the only way I could survive. I plunged ahead. "Howard, what happened?"

"We don't know yet, Becky," he shook his head. "At this point, all we know is that right after they took off from Rudy's Gliderport, they flew over the house to take some pictures. When Granddaddy Smith heard the plane, he walked out in the yard to wave. The plane circled overhead a couple of times, swooped down, then started soaring off. As it did, Granddaddy turned to walk in the house. He had only taken a couple of steps when he heard a loud noise. When he turned around and scanned the sky, the plane was gone. He saw it crumpled in the field near Mrs. Hines's house and started running as fast as he could.

"A man and his two boys were watching the plane as they drove along the road in front of the house. They saw it crash and stopped. Luckily they were with Granddaddy. It's a wonder he didn't die of a heart attack.

"Annie Lou Hines intercepted them at the gate to the field and wouldn't let Granddaddy get near the airplane. She was afraid it might catch fire and explode. She called the ambulance, rescue squad, then me at the office. I found Kat and by the time we got here, the rescue squad was already removing their bodies."

I cringed, listening to Howard. I had to know what happened, but oh how it hurt to hear it. I felt as if a swirling, murky nightmare was slowly sucking me into a darkness that I would never be able to escape. *God, where are you?* I cried silently. *Help me. Do something, please!*

"Here, honey, the doctor sent this to you," Kat said, offering me a pill in the palm of her hand.

"No, I don't want to take any medicine," I protested.

"At least take half of it. It will help relax you for a while," she said, breaking the pill in two pieces. "You've got to take it. You have not closed your eyes. You have not eaten. You can't go on like this. You must have strength for the days ahead. Please, will you take a little?"

Obediently I took the half pill from her hand and went to the kitchen for a glass of water. I learned long ago not to argue with Kat or Grandmother. They were the strongest individuals I had ever known, and now I would draw from that strength. I swallowed the pill and sat down again to talk with the Weavers. In a few minutes, my eyelids grew heavy. A weird sensation crept slowly over my whole body. "I think I'll lie down for a minute," I said. Making my way to the bedroom, I stretched out on the bed and fell asleep. For a moment, the terror faded.

Someone was shaking me, calling me, "Becky. The funeral home people will be here shortly. Can you wake up now?"

I opened my eyes to see Grandmother standing over the bed. For a moment I couldn't remember where I was. Seeing the anguish in her aged face brought me quickly back to reality. I sat up. It was nearly dark outside.

"Grandmother, where's Tonya?" I asked anxiously.

"She's still at Kat's house. They're bringing her home in a while."

I stood up and smoothed the wrinkles in my clothes. Hurrying to the bathroom, I washed my face and brushed my hair. By the time I made it to the den, the funeral home people had arrived. After the introductions, I sat rigidly in a chair and waited while the others made small talk.

In a few minutes, Joan arrived with Tonya, who was very tired. I tucked her in bed, stroked her hair and fingered the curls at the nape of her neck until she fell asleep. Then I returned to the den.

One of the men from the funeral home handed me two small brown paper bags. "Mrs. Smith, these are the personal items that belonged to your husband and son," he said gently.

"Thank you, sir," I said, opening one of the bags. Greg's billfold and the pocket knife Granddaddy had given him for Christmas were in it. I quickly closed the bag. I was not ready to look at the contents.

I peeked into the other bag and saw Sonny's billfold, checkbook and white gold wedding band. I slid my hand in the bag and eagerly snatched the ring. Holding it tightly, I rubbed my fingers along the chain grooves around the outer edges. I slipped it on my middle finger and tried to absorb a sense of Sonny's presence. I felt strangely comforted. Sonny was with me. Now I had a part of him I could hold onto.

Around ten that evening, the crowd began to dwindle. I eased to the phone in the hall and dialed Mike and Louise Corbett, college friends living in Nashville, Tennessee. Mike and Sonny had formed a band called the Vagabonds. Mike played lead guitar; Sonny, the saxophone. After we married, the four of us had lived in the same duplex, shared beans and chili and played Monopoly. Mike and Louise were forever friends.

Mike answered on the second ring and I said, "Mike, this is Becky Smith. How are you?"

"Becky, I'm fine. How in the world are you?"

"Mike, something terrible has happened. Sonny and Greg have been killed in a plane crash. I need you."

He was so stunned he couldn't speak. Finally he managed to ask, "Where are you now?"

"I'm in Florida, but I'll be going home as soon as the bodies are released."

"We'll be there waiting," he said. That was all I needed to know. I put the receiver in its cradle and walked through the kitchen to the den.

A while later we heard a knock at the front door, and when Grand-daddy Smith opened it, my family was standing on the porch. My sister Jerlene and her husband had driven Mama and Daddy down to be with us. They also brought along two of my nephews to drive my car home.

In an instant I flew straight into Daddy's and Mama's arms. We locked in a combined embrace. "They're gone," I sobbed. "Sonny and Greg are gone." We held each other and wept.

For the moment I felt like a little girl again. I had been hurt, and Mama and Daddy were here to make it better. They would hold me and let me cry. They would make the hurt go away. Then the force of reality overcame me; this time Daddy and Mama could never make it better. The hurt was so deep, the wound so invisible; how could anyone heal a hurt they could not see?

CHAPTER FIVE

Bitter or Better

ARLY the next morning, the Federal Aviation officials completed their preliminary investigation and released the
bodies. Now we could have the funerals.

Floy had decided to bury Jack and Richard nearby in the Smith family
plot at the High Springs Cemetery. Their funeral was scheduled for four
that afternoon at the First Baptist Church. Sonny and Greg were being
flown home to North Carolina. I was anxious that they not leave without me.

About midmorning Floy called. "Becky, I know it's a long trip home,
and you have many arrangements to make. If you need to go, I will certainly understand. Don't feel like you have to stay here for the funeral."

"Oh, Floy, thank you," I sobbed, my heart full of gratitude. I was not
sure I was strong enough to make it through two funerals. I still felt that
if I did not see their dead bodies, I might wake up to find that it had

only been a nightmare. I had not looked at the airplane, seen the caskets or identified the bodies. I had not yet come face to face with death.

"Floy, how are you doing?" I asked.

"I'm holding together. Right now nothing seems real. Becky, I just can't understand it. Jack and Richard were such careful pilots. Their flight logs were complete to the minutest detail. I'm sorry, so sorry," she cried softly.

"I know, Floy. Don't think about it now, and please don't worry about me. You have enough to deal with. If it's really all right with you, I think I'll start home. I've got so many details to work out before the funeral."

"Take care of sweet Tonya," Floy continued, "and I'll see you in Hendersonville. I don't know if Daddy and Mama will be able to make it through two funerals and the long trip; but Kat, Howard and I will be there."

When I hung up the phone, I felt ashamed that I was not as strong as Floy. She had been to the airplane and walked around in the wreckage. She had picked up her son's bloodstained jacket; her tears had mingled with his blood. She had been to the funeral home, picked out their caskets and made all the arrangements. She had taken care of Jack's mother and looked after her own parents. She had comforted both her daughters.

In contrast, I had done nothing but hide. Now it seemed as if I were deserting her by not attending the funeral. Yet I felt as if I, too, might die from the pain and hurt. I did not realize at the time that I was fluctuating in and out of the first two phases of grief—shock and denial. I did not know people react to death in different ways or that the paths of grief could go in opposite directions. I felt as if I were fighting for survival the only way I knew, which was to escape.

As my family and the Weavers prepared to leave Florida, I decided to ride home in my pastor's car. I knew I could stretch out in their back seat and not have to talk. Their son, John, rode with my nephews, and Tonya went with Mama and Daddy. Before we left, I called my friend Mary Ellen O'Shields and asked her to make sure no one was at my house when we arrived. I needed some time at home alone.

"Don't worry, Beck. I'll take care of it," she assured me. Mary Ellen had already responded to the newspaper reporters, supplied them with pictures they had requested and covered other numerous details for me.

Nine hours on the road gave me a lot of time to reflect. My mind raced across the thirteen-and-a-half years Sonny and I had shared together. It seemed it was only yesterday that we stood at the altar in Mount Olivet Church and repeated our vows before my uncle, Reverend Alva Ballard. We had a one-night honeymoon at the Holiday Inn in Asheville. The next morning we left for Rome, Georgia, our three-room duplex and our senior year at Berry College.

Berry offered a unique program that allowed us to earn our tuition. Sonny had worked in the orchard; my job was in the Alumni Office. We met and fell in love as sophomores, were engaged a year, then married the summer before our senior year. I graduated from Berry on Sunday, and Greg was born on Wednesday. We had started life together in a whirlwind and never slowed down.

Like most young couples, Sonny and I experienced a mixture of good times and bad. Early in our marriage, we learned how fragile life really is and how painful it is for parents to see their children suffer. Before Greg was nine months old, he was hospitalized twice, once for a blood disorder and the second time for pneumonia.

During our second Thanksgiving together, Sonny and I were packing the car to spend the holiday with my family in North Carolina when he suddenly clutched his chest and gasped, "Beck, I can't breathe."

I rushed him to the hospital emergency room. The doctors admitted him to the cardiac unit and immediately began running tests. The next morning Dr. Greene sat on the foot of the bed and explained, "Mr. Smith, I don't want to scare you, but it appears you may have suffered slight heart failure. Your heartbeat is strong, but we're baffled because the X-rays reveal a strange configuration in your chest. It looks like your heart is slightly out of place."

Heart failure? Sonny was only twenty-three years old. Dr. Greene did more tests and finally concluded that the sac surrounding the lung was inflamed, and the immediate problem was pleurisy. However, he recommended that Sonny go to the research hospital at the University of Florida for a complete medical check during summer vacation.

The following June, Greg and I stayed with Granddaddy and Grandmother Smith while Sonny checked into Shands Teaching Hospital at the University of Florida. For three weeks the doctors probed, studied and tested. Finally they concluded that Sonny's right lung had collapsed sometime during childhood. His left lung had enlarged to compensate for the air flow, shifting his heart out of place. The doctors determined that it wasn't a harmful condition; Sonny could continue his normal activities without any restrictions.

Now my Sonny is not breathing at all, I thought. *He will never breathe again. Oh, God, how could such a thing be?*

Riding home, my thoughts changed from memories that made me cry to memories that caused me to smile. I thought about our most special Christmas, the year Greg was six and Tonya, three. We were surviving on Sonny's paycheck as band director and the extra money I earned selling cosmetics part-time.

We had managed to buy our first home in Flat Rock, North Carolina. But we were still tunneling our way through the mountainous medical bills from Greg's and Sonny's hospital stays, so we found ourselves on a strict budget. I had learned to sew clothes, clip coupons and prepare ground beef 1,001 ways. We also ate lots of peanut butter and jelly sandwiches, but we did not feel deprived. More money would have made it easier; it would not have made us happier.

We wanted to make Christmas special for Greg and Tonya, but without money it was going to be a challenge. One day in early December, I saw an ad in the newspaper, advertising a garage sale that was offering children's toys. I called for directions, left Tonya at my sister's house and scurried across town. I selected as many toys as I could afford, loaded them in the car and raced home. By the time Sonny arrived home from school that afternoon, I had everything spread across the basement floor and was jumping up and down with excitement.

Every night after Greg and Tonya were in bed, Sonny and I hurried to the basement. We hammered, scrubbed, sanded and painted our love into the secondhand toys. The child-size table and chairs sparkled under a new coat of daffodil-yellow paint. The Chinese-red toy piano glistened. I lined the doll bed with soft white fake fur. Sonny scrubbed the pint-sized refrigerator until it gleamed. We could never get the stove rewired so it worked, but I knew Tonya's imagination could. Greg's bicycle looked almost new with its purple paint, a light reflector and an oogah horn.

Christmas Eve Sonny and I were giddy with excitement as we carefully placed each item under the Christmas tree. The next morning we had to make ourselves stay in bed until Greg and Tonya woke up. We even pretended to be asleep when they pounced on us.

In the living room we watched them run from one toy to the next; the delight in their eyes were all the joy Sonny and I needed.

When their excitement subsided, I reached back under the tree and pulled out the one last gift I had hidden. It was for Sonny. I just could not let Christmas pass without at least one tiny gift for him. Tears glistened in his eyes when he opened the package and saw the ninety-nine cent pair of socks and the two-dollar tie I had wrapped in tissue paper. He understood the love.

Suddenly he broke into a sheepish grin. "Wait here," he said, putting on his shoes and hurrying out into the cold, clad only in his pajamas and flimsy blue housecoat.

Shortly he reappeared at the door, holding something behind him. "Here, honey," he said, handing me a pea-green cardboard suitcase. Excitedly he explained, "This is for your cosmetics. I got it at Roses. The sign said it was a broken set. But I couldn't find a thing wrong with it!"

My heart swelled with love for him as I burst out laughing. "Honey, a broken set means the other pieces have been sold."

"It does?" he chuckled. "I knew this piece wasn't broken."

Later in the day, Kat and Howard called to wish us a Merry Christmas. I got on the extension phone.

"What did you get for Christmas?" Kat asked.

"Clothes," Sonny responded.

"What did you give Beck?"

"Oh, luggage," he replied. We both muffled a giggle.

As soon as we hung up, I exploded, "Clothes, luggage!"

We howled with laughter, but even as we laughed, I knew Sonny's pride was at stake. He did not want his family to know we were having a hard time financially. He wanted to provide for us, and I was determined to live happily with what he could provide. I would fiercely protect his pride. He was the man I loved with all my heart.

Now he was dead. I could not bear it. I just could not bear it. *Please, God, just let me die too,* I pleaded silently. *Life without Sonny would not be worth living.*

"Becky, you know, I've been thinking," Dean interrupted my thoughts. "This experience will make you bitter, or it will make you better."

As I mulled over Dean's statement, I knew he was right. I could become bitter, hostile and angry; or I could become better. Which would I choose?

In my heart, surrounded by darkness, riding in the back seat of my pastor's car on a lonely interstate highway near Athens, Georgia, I set the course for the rest of my life. No, I would not become bitter; I would become better. I would learn everything life had to teach me through this experience. I would be strong. I would survive, and I would become a better person because of it. The time had come for me to take charge.

CHAPTER SIX

Death Is Forever

A T the next rest stop, I called Dick and Ellie Buttner. Dick was president of the East High Band Booster Club. For the ten years Sonny had been band director, one of their three children—Sue, Rick or Doug—had been active in band. They were like family to us.

When Dick answered the phone on the first ring, I said, "This is Becky Smith, Dick. I'm on my way home. We're going to get there about one o'clock in the morning. I know that is late, but could you, Ellie and Sue meet me at my house? I need to talk with you."

"We'll be there," he promised.

Sue had been one of my original flag corps girls, the auxiliary marching unit I coached for Sonny's band. She had graduated from Wake Forest University and returned home to work. Now she helped me select and train the girls. She was devoted to the band kids and would be able to help me respond to their needs.

After we got back on the road, my thoughts turned to the band, to the precious young people Sonny and I loved so much. We had taken our last trip to a marching contest in Cleveland, Tennessee, only two months before. Our goal was to receive a superior rating from a panel of judges who evaluated the band's marching, maneuvering and special effects during a timed show.

The band kids looked forward to the trip as much as to the performance. We usually spent Friday night at the Holiday Inn in Cleveland. They enjoyed throwing each other in the motel pool, greasing door knobs and blasting each other with water balloons. Short-sheeting the beds or trying to slip from room to room after curfew without getting caught filled them with glee.

Thinking they were fooling us made their mischief even more delightful. We did not mind, since their jokes were harmless, and we knew they would be ready for their performance the next day.

That Saturday morning we awoke to overcast skies and a drizzling rain. About midmorning festival officials announced that marching was our choice. Many bands chose not to perform, but our kids were raring to go. At the motel they snapped to attention when Patsy Ross, the drum major, called, "Band Ten-Hut."

Their eyes sparkled with excitement; they were ready for inspection. What a picture they were—110 strong, with their shoulders back, feet together and heads held high. They wore black pants with white stripes, white jackets with green satin strips across their chests and matching satin waist sashes. Their black wide-brimmed hats were pinned up on one side with a silver star, and their freshly polished white shoes matched their immaculate gloves.

As Sonny, Sue and I watched them in review, we realized we were playing a part in molding their lives. The memories we shared would be a part of us forever. It was a moment of intense pride for us.

When Patsy called, "Band At Ease," a spirited bedlam broke loose.

After the buses arrived at the stadium, the rain increased. The band members nervously lined up at the gate to await their performance. In a few minutes, the announcer introduced them: "And now, all the way from Flat Rock, North Carolina, let's welcome the East Henderson High School Marching Eagle Band."

Just as the announcer finished, the heavens opened and torrents of rain drenched them. Patsy looked questioningly at Sonny. He nodded. She blew the whistle, and with their heads held high they marched on the field.

Wet flags wrapped around their poles. The majorettes could not hold onto their slick batons. The musicians had to dodge muddy spots on the field, but they did not miss a beat as they performed their well-rehearsed drills.

They marched off the field soaking wet. Their shoes squished with water and rain dripped from their expensive horns, but pride glowed in their faces. They had done their best, and when they broke rank, they shouted for joy. Sonny, Sue and I laughed and cried with them as they danced around us.

Back at the motel they quickly emptied out of the bus so they could celebrate. Sonny and I sat alone, cuddled on the front seat of the bus. "How did they do?" I asked.

He shook his head. "Honey, they overblew. They wanted to do their best, but they played too loud and lost their tone quality. They won't get a superior rating."

Sonny was disappointed, not of his kids' performance but for them. Gently I put my arm around him. I never loved him more or felt closer to him than I did at that moment.

The band didn't earn a superior rating, but that didn't take away the joy they felt because they had performed their best—and in a flooding rain. Now they faced the hardest task of all, giving up their band director. What could I do to help ease their hurt?

As we neared home, retracing the route Sonny, Greg, Tonya and I had so happily traveled just four days earlier, my heart began to race. I could hardly wait to get inside my house where it was safe and warm. When we turned off Highway 25 onto our street, the lights were on. The Buttners' car was in the driveway. Dottie and Ted, my sister and brother-in-law, were also waiting for us.

When we stopped, I jumped out of the car and hurried through the carport into the house. I struggled to shut out visions of Greg standing there with his tackle box and fishing pole. Inside, I stopped for a brief moment to take in the familiar, comforting smell of our home. Food and flowers, evidences of love and concern, were everywhere. The house was clean, and I was grateful Sonny and I had taken the Christmas tree down before we left.

Dottie, Ted, Dick, Ellie and Sue were waiting in the living room. We hugged each other and wept. "I'll be right back," I said, wiping tears from my face.

Walking down the hall to Greg's bedroom, I closed the door, turned on the light and looked around. Everything was just as he had left it. A self-portrait he had drawn in kindergarten hung askew on his bulletin board. His basketball lay in the middle of his new trundle bed. His trumpet sat on the floor beside his bookcase.

I walked over and looked at some of his treasures on the bookshelf: a stamp collection, pet rock, his leaf collection— which he had won first prize for—and the newspaper clipping with his picture. I picked up his rabbit's foot. "It wasn't too lucky, was it, honey?" I cried softly, fingering the soft white fur.

Slowly I turned, shut the door behind me and walked to Sonny's and my bedroom across the hall. I stepped inside and leaned against the door. Sonny's gold recliner was next to our bed. I pictured him sitting in it, Greg and Tonya cuddled on either side of him. Every Thursday night when I came home from graduate school, I would find them in his chair, eating popcorn and watching TV.

I sat on the edge of our old poster bed and caressed the knob at the top of the spindle. We had bought it at a secondhand furniture store when we moved from our apartment. I had painted it at least three different colors over the years. Gently I fluffed Sonny's pillow; he liked it that way.

I got up and opened his closet. I ran my fingers down the row of freshly laundered shirts and paused at his green-and-white-checked, sport coat. He wore it every time the band performed. It was his uniform. What memories it held.

Next I wandered over to the dresser and opened his underwear drawer. Being close to Sonny in a way only I knew him gave me strength. No one else in the world had shared the intimacy of this room. Finally I picked up a T-shirt, hugged it to me and put it back in the drawer. Then I wiped my tears and went back into the living room.

Mama and Daddy had also come. They were weary, so I insisted they go home to rest. Dottie and Ted put Tonya to bed and went to sleep, too. For a long time, Dick, Ellie, Sue and I sat in the living room and talked. They told me how they had first heard the news, their own stunned reactions, then those of the band kids and community. We decided that involving the band kids in the funeral might give expression to their grief.

Dick also told me how he was handling memorial funds that had already been designated for Sonny and Greg. Since I had requested no flowers, people who wanted to offer a memorial had been encouraged to send their contributions to the band. Dick had opened a special account. I felt good about what he had done and thanked him.

Just as the Buttners prepared to leave around two-thirty in the morning, Mike and Louise Corbett arrived from Nashville, Tennessee. We sat at the kitchen table, drank coffee and reminisced until daybreak. I heard myself talking about how Sonny used to laugh or how Greg used to walk. It seemed strange to hear myself talking about them in the past tense, because I still believed they would be coming home soon.

After Mike and Louise left for their motel to get some rest, I washed my face, brushed my teeth and lay across my bed still fully dressed. I drifted fitfully in and out of sleep.

About seven-thirty, I heard voices in the kitchen and realized it was Friday. I sat up on my knees at the head of the bed and raised the shade. A dense fog had enveloped the house. I was surprised to see the white ground. *Oh, snow,* I thought happily. *Sonny and Greg loved the snow. They would be so happy.*

Immediately my thoughts turned to all the things I had to do: pick a grave site, plan a funeral service, get ready for visitation and be emotionally prepared to respond to people who needed to express their grief.

By nine o'clock I had showered, shampooed my hair, put on makeup and dressed for the day. I was standing at the living room window drinking coffee, when a car pulled into the driveway. It was my friend, Mary Ellen. She brought her daughter Shannon to play with Tonya.

"Oh, goodie, now me and Shannon can play blindman's bluff," Tonya said. "Aunt Dot, can we go get Crysti and Tiffi?" Crysti and Tiffi were Dottie's two girls, both younger than Tonya.

"Sure, we can," Dottie replied.

My sister, Dottie, was five years younger than I. Growing up, she had been my little blonde-haired shadow. I had always felt fiercely protective of her, but now our roles were reversed. For once, I would have to lean on her, and I was grateful to have her near me.

"Isn't the snow wonderful?" I asked Mary Ellen.

"Beck, that's not snow. It's sleet, and it's very treacherous," she said.

"What do you need me to do today? I'm here to help you."

"Well, first I must go to the funeral home. I need to talk with Sonny," I said matter-of-factly.

She did not seem surprised or question what I had said. "Okay, I'm ready whenever you are," she replied.

"Before we go, let me call Daddy."

When he answered the phone, I said, "Daddy, the roads are covered with sleet, so I don't know when I can get on the mountain. Will you go ahead and pick out a grave site for me? I want it on the hill next to your family plot. And, Daddy, have the men put a vault in the ground, will you? I want Sonny and Greg protected as much as possible."

"I'll take care of everything," Daddy promised. "Don't you worry about a thing."

I knew he would.

I picked up my tan winter coat and turned to Mary Ellen. "I'm ready to go."

I knew I was about to make the longest trip of my life. As we inched our way along the Greenville highway, I tried not to think or feel, because I already knew what I had to do. When Shepherd's Funeral Home came into view, it seemed so hauntingly lonely amid the towering trees, icicles hanging from their branches.

As we got out of Mary Ellen's car, the misty rain chilled us. We cautiously inched our way along the ice-covered walk toward the massive white doors. An eerie silence hung in the air like the frozen icicles. Hesitantly, I touched the brass door knob.

Suddenly fear—fear of the unknown, fear of death—washed over me like a powerful wave in a roaring hurricane. I started to tremble and was overwhelmed by nausea. Taking a long, deep breath, I finally pushed open the door. An antiseptic smell mingled with the fragrance of freshly cut flowers. I wanted to vomit.

We stepped into the lobby area. Down the long hall, we could see several doors. Lighted stands, with a book and pencil on top of each one, were on the right side of each door. To our left was the business office.

An immaculately dressed gentleman approached. "May I help you?" he asked in a practiced voice.

"Yes, I'm Becky Smith. I've come to see my husband and son."

"Yes, ma'am. Right this way, please," he said, leading the way to the chapel as Mary Ellen took a seat in the lobby.

Trembling uncontrollably, I pushed opened the door slowly. Before me sat two, closed, steel-gray caskets. I gasped for breath.

"Which one is my son?" I whispered pleadingly, searching the funeral director's cold eyes.

"The one on the left."

"Thank you, sir," I said. "I want to be alone now."

Gently he closed the door. I stood motionless, staring at the caskets. They were so still. So silent. I could feel my insides coiling into knots. My mouth felt dry. Hot tears scalded my cheeks. I shivered as the room seemed to spin wildly. Each breath came in gasping, painful spasms. My rubbery legs would not move. Piece by jagged piece, I felt as if my heart was shattering. I could no longer deny the truth. At last, I had come face to face with death.

"Please, God," I begged, "please help me!"

I do not know how long I stood transfixed, gazing on the scene before me. Finally I forced my feet to move slowly toward the caskets. I stopped between them and stared for a long time. Kat had done a good job. The handsome caskets were almost identical.

Fearfully I reached out to touch Greg's. It was cold. Chills ran up my spine. Quickly I pulled back my hand. "Honey, this is Mama," I said aloud, touching it again, moving closer. "I just want to tell you, I love you. You're the very best son any mama ever had.

"We had some really good times together, didn't we, little buddy? Remember when Daddy scared you and your friend Sean with the hatchet man story that time at Myrtle Beach? I'll never forget seeing the two of you run from the woods with gray moss hanging all over you. You were scared silly."

As I talked, images of my little boy floated before my eyes. How I longed to gather his lifeless body in my arms, cradle him to my breast and tell him I loved him. Finally realizing I would never again know that joy, I lay my head on top of his cold, gray casket and sobbed. All the hurt and confusion of the past three days flooded over me in wave after pounding wave as pure agony poured from my soul.

When I could straighten up, I turned to Sonny. "Honey, I need to talk with you. I've got some decisions to make, and I need your help." I sat on the floor between the caskets and crossed my legs.

"Please, Sonny, tell me what to do. How am I going to get through the next few days? How am I ever going to live without you?" Time lost its relevance. I sat on the carpet, rambling until a sudden urge to touch Sonny almost overpowered me.

I got up and stood by his casket; a battle began to rage inside me. "Just lift the lid and touch him," a tiny voice whispered. I fingered the handle. It would be so easy.

"At least you could see him one last time," another voice said. "Then you wouldn't always have to wonder."

Do I dare lift the casket lid or do I leave it closed? What does he really look like? Was Howard telling me the truth? Are they both really still whole? All I had to do was raise the lid and see for myself. The thoughts raged back and forth, *Go ahead. No, don't. Go Ahead. No, don't.*

Finally, fear won. I was too afraid to see their faces, to look directly at death. Standing between those two, steel-gray caskets with sleet and rain misting outside Shepherd's Funeral Home chapel, I experienced the most hopeless moment of my life. I knew that nothing, not tears nor prayers, absolutely nothing, would ever bring Sonny and Greg back to me. They were gone. Never again would they breathe, walk, talk, laugh, see or feel. They were dead.

CHAPTER SEVEN

Saying Goodbye

AS Mary Ellen and I left the funeral home, I was haunted by how bare the caskets looked and how empty the room seemed without flowers. I kept thinking, too, of Sonny, dressed in his nice blue plaid jacket and pants but wearing his everyday crepe bottomed shoes. "Uglies," he called them. They would not keep his feet warm. I made a mental note to send some socks and his dress shoes back to the funeral home. Greg would need some, too. I did not want their feet to get cold.

"Mary Ellen, will you take some things back to the funeral home for me?" I asked. "I've also got to have something on the caskets. Could I just use a single, long-stemmed red rose and their Bibles?

"Why not?" she replied.

We stopped at Village Florist. Diana Houston, the owner, had once been a student of mine. She was making a bouquet of tiny yellow rosebuds when we entered the shop.

"This is for Greg," she explained. "Toni Wilson wanted him to hold it."

Tears sprang to my eyes. "Oh, Diana, the caskets will be closed. I'm sorry. Could we use them as a bouquet nearby?"

I was deeply moved by Toni's thoughtfulness. She was one of Greg's classmates. I was grateful she remembered him. People loved Sonny so much I feared they might forget my little Greg had died, too. After we left the florist, Mary Ellen and I drove up Mount Olivet to the graveyard, even though the roads were still icy. Daddy had chosen a beautiful spot on the hillside. The morning sun would keep Sonny and Greg warm.

When we finally arrived back home, Tonya met me at the door. "Mama, the phone has been ringing off the hook. Where in the world have you been?" she asked. "We've been worried about you."

"Mary Ellen and I have been taking care of some business, honey. We've been to the funeral home and up on the mountain to see the grave sites for Daddy and Greg. They're perfect." I gave her a hug and then said,"Thank you for helping Aunt Dot take care of things here."

"You're welcome," she said, running back to play.

I went immediately to put Sonny's and Greg's dress shoes and some clean socks in a paper bag. I found their Bibles, and when I opened them, I knew I had made the right decision. Greg's read, "To Greg Smith, From Daddy and Mama, December 25, 1977." He had died two days later.

Sonny's said, "To Marion Smith, From Becky, Greg and Tonya, December 25, 1974." Greg's and Tonya's signatures, in their childish handwriting, only made it more dear. Underneath our names, Greg had written in a curving arch: "To the best Daddy in the whole world."

Their Bibles and a single rose would be perfect on silk coverlets across the top of each casket. It was simple yet meaningful. I also decided to place a wall hanging between the caskets. I had cross-stitched the Serenity Prayer when Tonya was four and in the hospital with pneumonia. For three days and nights, while I kept a vigil over her bed, I worked on the prayer by Reinhold Niebuhr: "God grant me the serenity to accept the things I cannot change, courage to change the things I can, and wisdom to know the difference."

As I read and reread the words, I knew I would make this my prayer for survival. I could not change Sonny's and Greg's deaths. It was not in my power to give Jack or Richard life again. All the tears in the world could not undo the accident. I knew somehow, someway, I had to find the strength to accept what I could not change. I also knew that the answer for my life lay with God, but He seemed to have disappeared.

As Mary Ellen was leaving with the items for the funeral home, Sue Buttner arrived to help plan the service. Carefully we organized every detail, wanting it to be memorable and meaningful. When we finished, Sue left to communicate our desires to the ministers and funeral home personnel. It seemed such a lot to ask of my young friend.

That afternoon, as I prepared to go back to the funeral home to receive friends, I thought about how I had dreaded this moment more than anything else. I did not know if I were emotionally strong enough to handle it.

To make matters worse, Kat, Howard and Floy had not arrived as they had promised. When I called Florida, Joan assured me they had left early that morning. They were long overdue. At six-thirty that evening, I finally had to leave without them. Visitation was from seven to nine.

The line at the funeral home was long. For two-and-a-half hours, a steady stream of friends moved by the closed caskets to pay respects to Sonny and Greg and speak to Tonya and me. Their love was deep, their sorrow genuine. I was comforted by their words of concern; the touch of their hands was reassuring. I was grateful for their love.

When the last person had gone, I stood up and started for the side door. Stopping briefly to touch a wreath of yellow flowers beside the entrance, I suddenly felt my legs buckle, and I fainted. I awoke to the pungent odor of ammonia. Dottie was waving smelling salts under my nose.

"Wake up, Mama, wake up," Tonya said, patting my face. I saw fear in her eyes.

"I'm all right, honey," I assured her. "Right now I just feel a little weak." When I could finally stand up, Daddy, Mama, Ted and Dottie took us home.

Howard, Kat and Floy still had not arrived from Florida, and I tried not to panic. The Highway Patrol in Florida, Georgia and the Carolinas assured us that they had received no reports of an accident involving a gray Lincoln with a Florida license plate. All we could do was wait.

Meanwhile, other family members had arrived from Florida and were staying at the Old Mill, a vacation resort in our neighborhood. The owners, Mr. and Mrs. McManus, had offered them free housing. Their generosity overwhelmed me. Fred and Martha, Sonny's brother and sister-in-law, were bringing Granddaddy and Grandmother Smith the next day.

About three in the morning, Howard called. They had just arrived and had checked into the Dutch Inn. They had taken a wrong turn outside Atlanta and wandered for hours through the mountain back roads of Tennessee and western North Carolina. They had been on the road eighteen hours. I was just relieved that they had arrived safely.

Saturday morning at dawn, I sat alone in Sonny's rocker recliner, watching the morning light peep through the fog. I couldn't help wondering where I would get strength to make it through the day.

The funeral was scheduled for eleven at the First Baptist Church of East Flat Rock. By ten-thirty, all the members of both families had arrived and were ready to leave for the church. I put on my coat and started to walk out of the bedroom. Suddenly on impulse, I turned back, took Sonny's green-and-white-checked, sport coat off the hanger and hugged it to my breast. *This is as close to him as I'll ever get again,* I thought. Aching to be near him, a powerful wave of grief rolled over me.

I laid the coat over my arm and walked resolutely out the door. Tonya and I climbed into the back seat of the long, black limousine. Mama and Daddy, Granddaddy and Grandmother Smith rode with us, too.

Through the misting rain, the funeral procession wound slowly down Robert E. Lee Drive and turned right on Highland Lake Road. As we drove past Flat Rock Junior High, I hugged Tonya close, resting my chin on her head. She sat very still. We passed Hill's Grocery, crossed over the railroad tracks and stopped at the traffic light. Turning left, we moved slowly onto the Old Spartanburg Highway.

Just as the church came into view, I gasped for breath. I was totally unprepared for what I saw. For a moment I thought my heart might stop beating. Tears sprang to my eyes as the sight imprinted itself forever into my heart and mind. The entire East High Band, 110-strong, stood at attention on a grassy knoll in front of the church. They were dressed in full uniform, their shoulders were back, feet together and heads held high, as they watched Sonny's and Greg's caskets being carried into the church.

As the limousine inched past the band, my eyes moved swiftly from face to face, storing up images. When I got out, Sonny's checked coat still resting over my left arm, I took hold of Tonya's hand, and we made our way directly to the band. Tears spilled silently down their cheeks as they stood straight and tall in the misting rain.

I could not help remembering a similar time, only two months before, when they had performed in the rain. Still, I knew that no performance they had ever given could possibly match their efforts today. Silently I hugged Sue; Patsy Ross, the Drum Major; then Eddie Watkins and Doug Buttner, Band Captains.

"Thank you for being part of today," I said. "He loved you so much."

For a long, silent time we stood together, united by our love and tears for the one who had touched our lives. Slowly I turned to go inside. It was time. Strains of organ music echoed softly as Tonya and I started down the aisle. Suddenly I felt Howard's strong arms guiding me past the section filled with Greg's little school friends. We moved past weeping friends and relatives into the front pew.

Stay alert, Becky, I kept reminding myself. *You've got to remember every detail of this day. It's all you're ever going to have.* With every ounce of energy I could muster, I tried to concentrate on the service.

The Reverend Eugene Johnston, the local Methodist minister, prayed, then we all joined in The Lord's Prayer. Ronnie McCallister sang a song I had requested: "The things that I love and hold dear to my heart are just borrowed, they're not mine at all . . . ." *Sonny and Greg were never really mine,* I reminded myself as he sang. *God just loaned them to me for a little while.*

After the Reverend Harold McKinnish's eulogy, Russell Burrell, one of Sonny's students, played "Danny Boy" on the saxophone. The melody and the saxophone sound were so haunting; for a moment I was transported back to college days when I sat at the foot of a stage, watching Sonny perform with his musical group, the Vagabonds.

Oh, Danny Boy, the pipes, the pipes are calling
From glen, to glen and down the mountainside,
The summer's gone, and all the roses falling
It's you, it's you must go, and I must bide.

Then the church choir sang "Learning to Lean," and for the first time I noticed Sonny's place in the choir was vacant. Tonya squirmed beside me. I put my arm around her and pulled her close. "I love you," I whispered softly.

Glancing down the row, I saw Granddaddy and Grandmother Smith. They seemed so pitiful and frail. How could they survive such heartache? Four members of their family wiped out in a heartbeat—a son, a son-in-law and two grandsons.

Sweet Floy sat bravely beside them. I longed just to reach over and put my arms around her. She had not only lost her husband and son, she had also lost her baby brother. *Is there no limit to the pain a person can bear?* I wondered.

Dr. Weaver, my beloved pastor and friend, spoke next. Using the text of 2 Samuel 1:23, he often struggled to keep his own emotions in check. Afterward Jimmy Stokes played a trumpet solo, "My Jesus I Need You." Once again I closed my eyes, remembering Greg's excitement when we bought his trumpet. I could still see the happiness on his little freckled face.

When I opened my eyes, the band officers were coming forward one at a time; each one laid a long-stemmed red rose on the caskets. They alternated, one rose for Greg, one for Sonny. I nearly lost my composure when Sean, Mary Ellen's son and one of Greg's best buddies, moved forward to place the final rose on Greg's casket. *Not now, Becky, not now. Stay strong a little longer,* I kept cautioning myself.

Then the funeral home director appeared and stood stoically by our row of seats and motioned for us to rise. I tried to stand, but my legs wobbled. "She can't stand up," I vaguely heard Howard whisper as he grabbed me. Suddenly two strong arms scooped me up. It was Roscoe Green, Sonny's best friend from Florida. Once again, the world went black.

When I came to, I was in the limousine, and Dottie was waving ammonia under my nose.

"I'm all right now," I assured her, sitting up.

As the funeral procession moved out of the church yard onto the highway, cars fell in line behind us, and we inched up Mount Olivet in the misting rain. Sonny and Greg were making their final journey.

At the grave side, the band kids huddled shoulder to shoulder in front of the open graves as fog closed in around us. Dr. Weaver prayed one last prayer. It was time to lower the caskets, and I simply could not watch. Thoughts of the bodies I loved being placed in a dark hole and covered with dirt was more than I could bear.

I got up, took Tonya's hand and walked down the hillside to the church. We waited inside while the graves were being covered. I kept wondering if Sonny's and Greg's feet would stay warm. I hoped the socks and shoes would help.

It seemed unbelievable that only seven days before Sonny and I had sat in Mount Olivet Baptist Church and watched Tonya and Greg in the Christmas pageant. In fact, it seemed only moments ago I was a little girl myself, singing "Jesus Loves Me" and learning Bible verses.

Does Jesus really love me? I wondered. *Where is He now? Why did He take Sonny and Greg away? Why would He take the life of my child before he really had a chance to live? Is all I had been taught about God true?* A tiny doubt slithered into my mind and quietly began to gnaw at my faith.

After the graves were covered, we said our private goodbyes and reluctantly started down the mountain. Leaving Sonny and Greg behind in the fog and freezing cold made me sick.

Granddaddy and Grandmother Smith spent the night with me and slept in my bed. Long into the night, Howard, Kat and I pored over my finances, debts and earning power. They wanted to make sure I would be able to make it financially. Over and over, I felt grateful for my job teaching kindergarten. I would be able to earn a living for Tonya and me.

The next morning, we all ate at Perkin's Pancake House. Then Sonny's family left for their homes.

I still faced one more difficult task. I had to clean out Sonny's desk. The students would be returning from Christmas vacation the following day, and the band room would soon belong to someone else. Once again, I called Sue, and she came to pick me up.

"I can't find Sonny's keys," I explained, getting into the car. "They must have been lost in the crash. Maybe one of the coaches will be at the school and can let us in."

I braced myself once more for this painfully wrenching task. It was a job I wanted to do. The band room held keepsake mementos of Sonny's that I would treasure.

As we drove into the parking lot, I noticed the spindly trees he had planted outside the band room windows. In my mind's eye, I could still see the big pink sign the students had taped across those windows when Tonya was born: Congratulations Ma and Pa Smith.

Behind the band room and beyond the tennis courts, I could see the football stadium. We had spent countless Friday nights with the band and football team. The kids loved to tease Sonny. They had a favorite chant. One group would start clapping in rhythm and yell, "But can you be-bop?" Another group would answer, "Yeah, we can be-bop!"

To the kids, be-bopping was a dance old folks did. When they started the chant, Sonny would grin, snap his fingers and shuffle his feet like he was dancing. They loved it.

Every nook and cranny of East High was crammed with memories for me. I had been in the first graduating class. As a student council officer, I had helped select the eagle mascot, name the annual, compose the Alma Mater and choose the green-and-white school colors. East High was a part of who I was.

Sue and I got out of the car and started up the steps to the band room.

For the first time, I looked up at the green double doors in front of me and froze. The doors were padlocked. A monstrous chain had been wrapped through the handles and secured with a lock. I was stunned. Why would anyone want to padlock the band room?

"We'll just have to go to the principal's house and get a key," Sue said.

We made the trip, secured the key and returned to the band room. As Sue opened the outside door. I held my breath as I walked into the hallway. I expected to hear the mixture of tooting horns and the rat-a-tat-tat of drums. My heart raced as I anticipated the sight of Sonny on his director's stool.

I trembled as we pulled open the door and stepped into the band room. The room was empty. Sonny's stool stood vacant in front of the tiers of empty chairs and music stands. No students. No music. No sounds— only a deadly, unfamiliar silence.

Quickly I scanned the room. On the wall behind his stool, the stereo equipment sat silent. The jazz album that I had bought Sonny for Father's Day, at the Smithsonian Institute earlier that summer, was on top of the stereo. Plaques and pictures of award-winning band performances hung on the wall. Near the door, on the far wall, the uniforms were hanging neatly in their closets. Sonny's desk was hidden behind the piano.

The air in the room was stale. I hurried across the room, but when I reached his desk, I came to a sudden stop. Someone had already been there. His belongings were strewn across the top of his desk. A picture of Greg and Tonya had been knocked over. The drawers were hanging open; papers stuck out in disarray.

Shock and anger surged through me like a wildfire. Sonny's desk was private.

"How could anyone be so cruel?" I cried as I eased down in his chair and looked at the mess in front of me. "What in the world were they looking for?"

"I don't know," Sue answered quietly, patting me on the shoulder reassuringly.

I picked up the picture of Greg and Tonya. They were smiling at me. Tonya was three and had on a long pink dress I had made for her. Greg wore an orange T-shirt from his first grade basketball team. I remembered how Sonny swooped him up into a bear hug after he scored his first two-point goal. After the game, we went out for hot fudge cake and ice cream to celebrate.

Sonny had been a terrific daddy. Now his little girl would have to grow up without him, and I would not even be able to give her a memento from his desk. Someone had spoiled it. I felt as if his things had been contaminated. Suddenly I could not wait to leave. I felt as if the walls were closing in. I raked the desktop items into boxes and said to Sue, "Let's go."

As we hurried out, I knew I could never again return to Sonny's band room. I felt sick and violated.

CHAPTER EIGHT

Vacant Days

WHEN *I arrived home, my house was still full of people. In a daze, I walked through the living room and down the hall,* nodding to those I passed. I did not want to think, feel or remember anymore. Just for a little while, I wanted to blot out life altogether. I made it to the bedroom, shut the door and leaned against the wall with my eyes closed. I took a long, slow, deep breath. At last, everything was over.

I had made it through the funeral with dignity. Somehow I had been able to concentrate on the details of what had to be done as each decision arose. The funeral service had been a lovely memorial to Sonny and Greg. I had been as strong as I could be. Now I felt paper thin and wasted. I just wanted the world to go away.

I opened my eyes and walked directly to Sonny's rocker-recliner beside our bed. As I sat down and began to rock, I gave way to the murky nightmare which had been swirling around me since I heard Joan say, "There's been an accident in the airplane." Slowly it sucked me into its terrorizing blackness. Not wanting to think or feel, I floated lifelessly in a dark void.

About midnight, Dottie gently knocked on the door. "Beck, why don't you take a hot bath and try to get some rest?" she urged.

"Is Tonya asleep?"

"She's in her bed," she assured me. "A hot bath might help you sleep, too."

After Dottie filled the tub, I gratefully settled into the hot, soothing water. For the first time in six days, I realized how weary I was and how little I had slept or eaten. My body felt like it had been wired with surging electrical currents that jolted and jarred me through the days and nights. I had not realized shock and fear were such propelling forces.

For a long time I just lay soaking in the hot, soapy water as I studied the new pink, blue and green striped wallpaper. Sonny and I had been putting it up before Christmas, but we had not had time to finish it. The wall behind the commode was still bare. I wondered what I was going to do now? I probably would not have the money to hire someone to hang the rest of the paper for me.

How was I going to stretch my paycheck to cover all our bills? Like an adding machine, a tape of figures began to click through my mind— house payment, car payment, insurance premiums, fuel to heat the house, water, telephone and electric bills, credit card debts, gasoline, groceries and clothes. I also needed money to cover Tonya's dancing lessons and costumes. I felt overwhelmed. For the first time ever, I understood the frustration Sonny must have experienced when we tried to juggle our needs and wants.

I soaked in the hot water until my skin began to shrivel. Finally I got out and dried with the fluffy pink towel Dottie had laid on the vanity.

As I hung the wet towel on the rack beside the sink, I noticed the wallpaper seam under the towel bar and smiled. Sonny thought his idea to hide it was clever. He had admired his handiwork and joked, "No one will ever notice it, Beck. It will be our secret."

Best friends always share secrets, I thought. *How would I ever survive without my best friend? How could I go on living with all the memories pasted on the walls, hanging in the closets or tucked away in every drawer?*

For the first time since the accident, I prepared to climb into Sonny's and my bed. As I pulled back the covers, a shiver surprised me. I unzipped my housecoat and laid it across the chair. Hesitantly, I sat on the side of the bed and turned off the lamp. Only the sounds of my own ragged breathing broke the deadly stillness as darkness surrounded me.

Slowly I lay back and swung my feet off the floor, tucking them between the sheets. My head sank into the softness of the foam pillow. For a moment I lay very still. Then from deep within me, an agonizing groan bubbled up and erupted. The empty space beside me took my breath away.

For a long time, I lay like a corpse in the darkness, afraid to move. My heart pounded so violently, I felt as if it might burst through my chest. Each heartbeat sounded like the blast of a cannon in the deadly stillness. Fear knotted my stomach and coiled around my body like a boa constrictor suffocating its victim. I felt it squeezing me tighter and tighter.

I ached to reach out and touch Sonny, but fear of the emptiness kept my hand frozen to my side. Painful thoughts whizzed around my head like cars on the Indianapolis race track. *He'll never sleep here again. He does not exist anymore. He quit breathing. He's gone. He is no more.*

I grabbed the sides of my head as if trying to catch the thoughts racing around inside. *Where is my Sonny now?* His precious body was lying on "Ballard's Mountain" in a six-foot-deep grave covered with dirt. I could not bear it. I just could not bear it!

Stop it, Becky. Don't think like this, I ordered myself.

Quickly I bounced out of bed, snapped on the light and stared back at the wrinkled sheets. The bed seemed to be my deadly enemy. Finally I sat down in Sonny's recliner, pulled the blanket off the bed and covered my feet.

I simply could not understand how someone so alive and vibrant could completely cease to exist from one breath to the next. How could life be so fragile? "Please, God, won't you help me?" I whimpered.

The next few days became dark, gaping holes. I remember little about them. School re-opened after the holiday break, but I did not return. I kept Tonya home with me. I vaguely knew that my family hovered close by. I was also aware that Dottie and Ted were there day and night, caring for Tonya. Mama and Daddy dropped by often. They greeted loving friends who continued to call, but they demanded nothing of me. Tonya always hovered protectively near me. She brought me hot coffee and got upset when people tried to make me eat. I found the sight and smell of food nauseating.

Mike and Louise Corbett, our college friends, stayed as long as they could. Before they left, Mike asked if he could clean out Sonny's truck and make sure it was ready for winter. I knew he understood the special bond between Sonny and his olive-green Chevy truck. I watched from the bathroom window upstairs as Mike drove the truck to the back of the house and parked it under a giant oak tree.

Mike stepped out of the truck, zipped his brown-leather jacket up to his chin, stretched a knitted cap over his head and pulled on black leather gloves. Reaching inside the cab, he took out a bucket of hot soapy water and a bristle brush. He bent down and started furiously scrubbing the right front tire.

Occasionally Mike took off his glasses and brushed away tears with his coat sleeve. I watched him raise the hood, change the oil and add some antifreeze to the engine. He vacuumed the cab, then swept out the camper with a broom. Finally he closed the camper cover and locked it. His job was complete.

Suddenly Mike leaned against the truck, buried his head in his arms and sobbed aloud. Deep, gut-wrenching, manly sobs. Quickly I turned away. His grief was private.

My days and nights blurred into each other. Often I sat alone in my bedroom or wandered in and out of Greg's room, picking up his treasures or rearranging the clothes in his drawers. Sometimes I would just lie on his bed and stare vacantly at the ceiling, listening for the sound of his voice.

I wondered, too, about the strange noises Greg told us he heard in the attic at night. We had brushed it off for a while, teasing him about his imagination. We even made up stories about the gremlins who lived in the attic. Finally he convinced us that he really was hearing something. Sonny thought a field mouse might have squeezed in through a vent, so he and Greg set traps. Now I wondered if a poor mouse had been caught in a trap and had frozen to death.

Nights for me were black with terror. Sleep was fitful and full of fear when it came at all. Each time I tried to lie down, I found myself clinging desperately to my side of the bed, rigid and afraid to move. Sonny's empty place seemed to claw at me in the darkness. It was so frightening to reach out for his warm body and find only emptiness.

Often I would awaken to find myself searching for him. I had felt so safe and secure in his arms. Now I recoiled in horror as I clutched the empty air. I dreamed of his arms around me. Now those arms had no life and were beyond my reach.

I simply could not comprehend that Sonny no longer existed, that he had disappeared from the face of the earth. In one breath, he was alive and vibrant, the center of the universe for me. In the next breath, he had become part of eternity. He was gone, but I did not know where. He just ceased to exist. Death was absolutely too incredible for me to comprehend.

The second week in January snow began to fall, blanketing the mountains and bringing a temporary halt to routine activities. The school buses were unable to travel on the gravel country roads, so the schools were forced to close. I was grateful for the extra healing time.

I frequently stood at the windows in the living room and watched the snow fall. I waited expectantly for Greg to dart from beside the house, snowball in hand, ready for a fight. Sometimes, such memories flooded me with great warmth; at other times, they brought pain.

When the memories became too painful, I would stuff them back in my little heart box and slam the lid. *I'll think about them later,* became my permanent way of coping. Picturing Sonny or Greg in my mind was so painful, I had to completely block them out. I hid all the pictures in the house except the ones on the living room wall of Greg and Tonya. Those pictures were special.

Tonya had been in kindergarten; Greg was in third grade. They had won a talent show at Hillandale Elementary School. They had also participated in Hendersonville's Fabulous Fourth of July celebration. They danced a mountain clogging routine to John Denver's song, "Thank God I'm a Country Boy."

I had made their matching outfits. Tonya wore a red, white and blue gingham dress which stood straight out over layers of ruffled petticoats. Her long auburn hair was tied in ponytails with blue and red ribbon. Greg wore a gingham shirt under his denim farmer overalls. For the picture, he had tucked his thumbs inside the shoulder buckles and put on his best mischievous grin.

The pictures were precious to me. Sometimes I would stand, stare at them and trace Greg's face with my finger. I vowed never to let time rob me of the only thing I had left of him, my memories.

Occasionally I would run my finger up and down the seams of the green-and-melon-striped wallpaper underneath the pictures and remember the little spat Sonny and I had over getting it hung. He had started wallpapering one evening, but after three months had only finished half the wall. I reminded him often how tacky it looked.

One night he became irritated with me for nagging him. I went on to bed without him. About three that morning, I awoke to find him furiously hanging paper down the hall. I got up, fixed a pot of coffee and teased him about getting upset. We sat on the living room floor, laughed and made up. How silly it seemed now to get upset over something as insignificant as wallpaper. If I had him back for just a fleeting moment, I would hug him, tell him how much I loved him and assure him it did not matter if he ever finished the paper. What mattered most was simply having him.

Getting dressed each morning became a major task for me. Just showering and shampooing my hair sapped my energy.

One day I plopped down on the couch with a towel wrapped around my wet hair. Staring at the woods across the road, I tried not to remember how often I had watched Greg and Tonya play in their hideout tucked away in the trees. They loved playing in the woods, especially in the springtime when the leaves began to unfurl and wildflowers bloomed. Their hideout was a natural garden of delicate pink lady slippers, a wildflower from the orchid family. Every spring we waited breathlessly for the first sign of the fragile, shoe-shaped blooms to appear. We thought of them as God's little surprises, hidden in shady, out-of-the-way places to brighten the forest. We pretended the lady slippers were the homes of magical fairies, and we tiptoed around them, careful not to bruise or destroy a single one. Lady slippers were our symbol of hope, hope for new life in the spring.

On that bleak, cold January day, snow was banked in the crevices of the naked tree branches, and it seemed spring would never come again. Green leaves would never unfurl, nor would the lady slippers ever bloom anymore. My world could never be the same. Greg was dead.

My thoughts were interrupted by the sounds of our church choir, singing, "Jesus, we just want to thank you. Thank you for being so good."

Ha! I thought bitterly as the music echoed from the tape recorder. *If Jesus is so good, why did He let Sonny and Greg die?*

Suddenly Sonny's strong tenor voice pierced the air, "Jesus, I just want to thank You."

I shot up and frantically grabbed the recorder from Dottie's hand as she tried to shut it off. "No, no," I pleaded. "Let me hear it again."

For a long time, I played the tape over and over, drinking strength from the sound of Sonny's voice. I had not heard it since he kissed me goodbye and said, "Bye, Babe, I love you."

The more I listened to him sing, the stronger I felt. His voice gave me renewed hope. I almost felt as if he might shuffle into the room any minute, grin at me and say mischievously, "Hey, Beck-a-doo!"

Except for the arrival of the mail, the days seemed vacant. I found great comfort in the cards, letters and notes that arrived daily. I was especially grateful when someone mentioned Greg. I was fearful those who grieved so deeply for Sonny would somehow forget my little boy had died, too.

His kindergarten teacher wrote, "He will be a 'star' for certain." Another friend lamented, "Your loss is my loss also." His sixth grade teacher remembered Greg as "a very special pupil [with] such outstanding principles, he stood out in the classroom." Her kind words were keepsakes for my heart.

The multitude of notes and letters also made me realize I was not alone in my grief. Letters of love and tribute poured in from Sonny's former students. People whose lives he had touched now reached out to embrace Tonya and me.

Martha Ragan Huggins's letter typified so many:

I, for one, will not forget him, because each time I hear a drum roll and see a band marching or hear voices singing in harmony, I will remember his smile and the labor of love he gave to his work, his community, and his family. Nothing, not even Death itself, can take away the memories, for they are ours always to keep.

Martha's letter made me think deeply about the influence we have on each other's lives. It reinforced my growing realization that we only have a brief time to make a meaningful contribution to the lives of those in our circle of influence. It truly is the only legacy we can leave behind. The investment we make in the lives of others is really all that matters.

Sonny had made a rich investment. Greg had so little time. *God, I don't understand it. It just isn't fair,* I screamed silently.

Sometimes people would enclose a gift of money or an offer of help. One dear friend, Myrtle Hawkins, sent a book of stamps with a note saying she wanted to help and thought the stamps might come in handy for the many thank-you notes I would be writing. It was a thoughtful surprise and, of course, I used the stamps.

I had another special friend who left her touch lingering on my life in countless ways. She was my spiritual mom, Lula Mae Briggs. Almost every day I received a handwritten note. "God's little love notes," she called them.

I found great comfort in Lula Mae's honesty. She did not offer any answers. She did not spout platitudes or tell me to be strong. All she could do was cry out to God in anguish, just as I was. There was one major difference, however—she believed He heard and answered. I was no longer sure. In one note, she wrote:

Of course, my human reaction immediately was, 'Oh, God, this just cannot be. Here is a precious couple, so very much in love, with two lovely children and who constantly give to others. Why, God, why, God?'

With these human reactions, I knew I needed the Scriptures, so I picked up my Bible and read and read and read, so that my mind and heart would not dwell on the human reactions of why but enable me to refresh my heart and mind on God. Faith only takes hold when we bury ourselves in God's Word, which has the answers to all our whys.

I have, moment by moment, put your name and Tonya's to God over and over again. 'Please, God, help Becky and Tonya. Please God, help Becky. Surround her with your presence, your comfort, your strength, your wisdom, your deepest love, and somehow give her an increased faith to look to you in this hour of great trouble.'

I was confident Lula Mae knew a real God. For years, I had watched her life. I knew she walked in God's presence, and I needed desperately to believe there was a God who loved me, that He was real, and that He cared about my pain. I wanted to believe He would help Tonya and me.

I needed Lula Mae to pray for me, because I could not pray for myself. It seemed the heavens were shut tight. Lula Mae became God's protective arms around me. I did not know then that this is how God loves us—through the real arms of His children.

CHAPTER NINE

Hard Lessons

I began to feel as if my mind resembled the airplane wreckage scattered over that field in Florida, with my thoughts often colliding and splintering into fragmented ruins. I would try to sustain a conversation but lose a thought in mid-sentence. I would open the front door and could not remember where I was going.

Inside, I felt dead and strangely detached from my own body. I felt as if the real me had disappeared, leaving skin and bones which had a life of their own. I wondered how a dead person could breathe or feel.

One day, as I sat on the couch, lost in this frightening, shattered world, I watched my right hand caressing my left arm. I pulled at the strands of fine blonde hair then gazed at the blue veins ridging up in my hands. I squeezed my arm gently, then picked up some skin between my thumb and forefinger and pinched hard. It hurt. I was startled.

"Okay, Becky," I said aloud. "You are not hurt physically. You are still in one piece. You've got to get up now and take charge of your life."

Struggle as I might, however, I could not seem to take charge. I felt powerless, desolate, as helpless as a baby. Death had robbed me of all control. But life still had many hard lessons to teach me.

My first one arrived quickly. I soon discovered life goes on. The sun still rose in the East every morning and set in the West every evening. Night followed day. People resumed their lives. Routine returned.

I often wanted to shout, "Hey, world, don't you know nothing is the same anymore? Sonny and Greg are dead! How dare you go on?"

Although others grieved with me and imagined what I was going through, they were unable to crawl inside my skin and feel what I was feeling. They observed my pain, but they could not take it and make it their own. And I could not turn off the hurt inside me. Nothing could make pain not be pain.

Even in the fog of shock, I knew life had to continue, especially for Tonya. January the tenth she turned nine, so we planned a birthday party. She wanted to have a skating party with a group of family friends who often celebrated happy times together.

At the Skyland Skating Rink, we all put on our skates and whizzed around the floor to the blaring sounds of "Bad, Bad Leroy Brown." To Tonya's delight, we celebrated with cake and ice cream, party hats and whistles. We all tried hard to pretend life was normal.

The following day a group of thoughtful mothers from our church surprised her with another party at McDonald's. I watched as she and her little friends giggled, whispered and ran around the tables, just as they always had. I was grateful for the love of our friends. She needed that kind of normalcy in her life.

Soon after Tonya's birthday, a letter arrived addressed to her. It was from Mrs. Yvonne Allen, her teacher from the previous year. She wrote, "Occasionally in life we are fortunate enough to meet extraordinary people. Those people go about our world making it a better place in which to live. The people whose lives they touch are made better by having known them." She went on to say that Tonya had been blessed with such a father and a brother. Mrs. Allen closed by saying, "The hurt, my darling Tonya, is deep. The memories are so many and so beautiful. Hold them close to your heart and meet life with a smile on your beautiful face and a song in your heart. Let that be your special gift to these special people in your life."

I was deeply touched by Mrs. Allen's sensitivity. She had once told me Tonya would someday light up the world. I knew her love and concern were genuine. After Tonya read the letter, I tucked it away. It was a keepsake she would treasure as she grew older.

Every day I studied Tonya's reactions and watched her at play. I listened closely for clues to what she was thinking and feeling. I was concerned about her growing sense of responsibility about me, but I did not yet realize the fear she was hiding. One minute she had a daddy and a brother; the next minute they were gone. She was not sure at what moment I might disappear, too.

The January snows continued, keeping the schools closed for an indefinite period. One day, I impulsively decided to go back to Florida. I needed to see Grandmother and Granddaddy Smith. Sonny would want me to take care of them. I packed a suitcase, and within hours, Tonya and I were on a Greyhound bus bound for Florida. We rode all night. Sonny's brother Fred picked us up in Jacksonville early the next morning.

When we arrived at the Smiths', Grandmother had a hot breakfast of scrambled eggs, bacon and fluffy biscuits awaiting us. In her typical fashion, she forced herself to carry on, doing the things she had always done to love us. She could not, however, hide the weariness of grief in her eyes or the tremble in her hands.

What a role model Grandmother Smith had been to me through the years. I loved her as though she had given me birth. I had never been just a daughter-in-law to her; she had made me her daughter. Now I longed to help her and to give back some of the love she had given so freely to me.

Granddaddy Smith was almost immobilized with grief, tortured with questions of "if only." "If only I hadn't gone into the yard. . . .If only I had gone with them instead of staying behind."

Having Tonya and me with them seemed to help. During the next several days, we spent a great deal of time talking and grieving together. Kat, Howard and Fred helped me piece together the sequence of events I had blocked out of my mind. By now, most of the airplane wreckage had been removed, and I found myself anxious to walk over the site.

One windy afternoon, Granddaddy, Grandmother, Fred, Tonya and I bundled up in coats and hats and walked across the field to the place where Sonny, Greg, Jack and Richard had died. I steeled myself against the feelings. Like the funeral, it was another one of the things I felt I had to do.

For a long time, the five of us wandered around the charred ground, lost in our own private world of thought. Fred was using a metal detector and suddenly reached down to pick up a shiny silver ring with a turquoise stone. It had belonged to Richard. The band was broken in half at the back.

How could such a thing happen? I wondered. *Was the impact that violent? Did Greg know what was happening as the plane spiraled downward?* Suddenly his little face flashed before my eyes. I could see terror in his eyes as he frantically grabbed for Sonny and screamed, "Daddy, Daddy!"

Vigorously I shook my head, trying to block out the horrifying thoughts. The hurt was too intense. I had already discovered that blocking out painful images was the only way I could cope.

Before we left the site, I bent down, picked up a broken piece of the airplane and tucked it inside my coat pocket. As we walked away, I ran my fingers over and over the jagged edge. It seemed so sad to me that this tiny piece of metal was all I could take away from the place that had taken so much away from me. I felt angry, bewildered and confused.

When it was time for Tonya and me to start back to North Carolina, Granddaddy and Grandmother Smith took us to the bus station in Gainesville. Just being near them had renewed my strength. I had drawn from their wisdom and soaked in their love. "Becky, all of us have to be strong. We've got to go on. We have no choice. Take care of yourselves and don't worry about us. Call and let us know you're home safely," Grandmother said, hugging us goodbye once again.

"Call us if you need us, honey," Granddaddy whispered, squeezing a twenty-dollar bill in my hand and folding my fingers around it. Tears trickled down our cheeks as a new bonding took place between us. I knew I was now sharing in a long-standing, unspoken ritual he had shared with his son.

Tonya and I arrived in Hendersonville just ahead of another heavy snowstorm. Ted, Dottie, Crysti and Tiffi picked us up at the bus station. It was the eighteenth of January.

"It's Daddy's birthday, and Mama said we could buy him a cake," Tonya announced as we started home. "Can we stop at McFarlan's Bakery, Uncle Ted?"

"You bet," he replied.

She picked out Sonny's favorite, a carrot cake. The clerk wrote, "Happy Birthday, Daddy" in orange icing.

At home once again, we celebrated, trying to pretend life was normal. But I discovered what widows before me already knew--the pain that comes after a death, facing those special occasions for the first time without the one you love. There are no words, there just aren't any to describe the overwhelming sense of loss and sadness. The carrot cake tasted like ashes in my mouth.

A few days later, Dottie called. They were planning to go shopping in Spartanburg, South Carolina. "Why don't you and Tonya ride with us?" she asked. "The main highways have been cleared."

"Okay," I agreed.

When they came to pick us up, I asked if we could stop by the post office. Sifting through a handful of mail, I spied a manila envelope and quickly tore it open. Inside I was flabbergasted to discover a life insurance policy on Sonny. As I examined it, I vaguely remembered him telling me he had taken out a small policy in November. He had signed up for it with a payroll deduction.

When we got back home, I examined his bank statement and discovered that only one premium had been deducted. I was not sure the company would honor the policy. When I called to inquire, however, they assured me it was valid.

After I filed the necessary forms, they responded promptly. I felt guilty accepting the money, almost as if somehow I were being unfair to them. I was grateful, however, not only for the small amount of money but for their professional courtesy. My first lesson in the business world had been an easy one.

New responsibilities rested heavily on my shoulders. I realized no one could do them for me. My first task was finding an attorney who could lead me through the maze of fulfilling the legal requirements for settling Sonny's estate. On the recommendation of a friend, I made an appointment with Boyd Massagee, a Hendersonville attorney. Ted came to drive me through the snow to the attorney's office.

I found Mr. Massagee to be both professional and compassionate. A bond of trust immediately developed between us. By phone I introduced him to Howard, my brother-in-law in Florida. Howard is a business-man, and I knew he would protect my interests. He knew what Sonny and I owned and what we owed. I also knew he would be able to think clearly when I might not. As I left Mr. Massagee's office, I felt secure, but I also realized I had a lot to learn.

Before long, I discovered the value of a will. Sonny and I did not have one. If we had made out a will, we would have decided together what should be done about our property and our children's care. We could also have done it without the emotional trauma I now felt, making such critical decisions alone.

I soon learned a great deal about inheritance, property and tax laws. They vary dramatically from state to state, and I found out how impor-tant it is for a woman to be informed of her legal rights and respon-sibilities. I discovered, too late, the value of an insurance policy on our home mortgage. It would have automatically paid off the loan for our home, but we did not have it.

Adequate life insurance for Sonny and me was also something we had considered a luxury. It would have taken money we needed for shoes and clothes and had become an item we continually postponed. Had Sonny and I died together, I was distressed to discover a judge would have decided where and with whom Tonya and Greg would have lived. How foolish we had been not to have designated someone to be their guardian.

But of course, we never thought about dying. It was something that happens to old people—to other people, not to us. We were young. Sonny was thirty-five. I was thirty-four. Life was ahead of us. Death was never a part of our thoughts or plans.

One of the things I found most valuable was my own checking ac-count. I was a member of the Business and Professional Women's Organization, and I already knew how important it was for a woman to

85

have an established line of credit. If I had not had credit when Sonny died, I could have had difficulty gaining it on my own.

I was also shocked to learn that the way Sonny's and my names appeared on a joint bank account would affect the availability of funds. If our joint checking or savings account had read Mr. *and* Mrs. Marion O. Smith, then all assets in the account would have been frozen until the estate was settled. In this case, I might not have had enough grocery money. Although I would not have been able to touch the money we needed to live on, the bank would have continued to deduct its monthly service fee. Fortunately, our account read Mr. *or* Mrs. Marion O. Smith, and I had no problems obtaining funds.

Another reality I had to face, all too soon, was funeral expenses. They were staggering—perhaps more so than might be expected, since two funeral homes in two different states were involved. I knew I would have to pay airfare to have Sonny and Greg flown home, but I was surprised to discover itemized charges for a guest book, note cards, limousine services, telephone calls, overpriced overlays for the caskets, a fee for the use of the parking lot, a charge for the chapel used during visitation and numerous other things I had not requested.

I had chosen to pay extra for airtight vaults to protect the caskets—an unnecessary expense for the country church cemetery, but an important one for me. It seemed such a little thing I could do to protect Sonny and Greg.

The bills might have been even higher had Kat and Howard not guided me during this vulnerable time. They kept me from making devastating financial decisions in my emotional desire to provide what I considered the best for Sonny and Greg.

As all of the new responsibilities weighed me down, grief continued to consume my whole being. I was not capable of making sound decisions. I could not think clearly. I felt as if I were lost in a thick fog and could not find my way home. I was terrified. Such, I discovered, was the way of grief.

The most important question I had to settle in my own heart was where Sonny and Greg were. I wrestled with it continuously. I longed to be near them, but fear kept me from going to their graves. In fact, I could not even visit Daddy and Mama, because I had to pass the graveyard to get to their house. Thoughts of Sonny's and Greg's bodies covered by mounds of dirt sent chills racing through me. I would not allow myself to think about what was happening to their precious flesh.

I questioned myself unmercifully. Did I really believe what I had been taught about heaven and hell? Was there life after death? Did we have souls? What was a soul anyway? I felt as if my very survival depended on finding answers to the questions tormenting me.

Voraciously I began to read every book or magazine article I could find that dealt with these subjects. I haunted the bookstores and libraries, searching for something to help me understand. I begged people for answers.

I tried to read my Bible, but I was grieving so deeply I found it difficult to follow the thee's and thou's of *The King James Version*. Someone suggested I try *The Living Bible*. I bought one and found it easy to read. Eagerly I searched the Scriptures for answers. I felt desperate for some assurance that death was not the end of it all.

One day my pastor and his wife stopped by for a visit. Dr. Weaver saw a book someone had left. It was written by a lady who claimed she had gone to heaven and returned.

"Whose book is this?" he demanded.

"I don't know. Somebody brought it to me."

"Well, Becky, I'm going to take it with me. If they ask for it, tell them I have it," he replied sternly. "You don't need to read things like this. It will confuse you."

His reaction disturbed me, but I knew he felt deeply protective, and I appreciated his concern. I also realized that I was confused and gullible and an easy prey for unsound doctrine. I knew he had sent up a warning signal.

The book I found most comforting was a devotional called *Streams in the Desert: Volume I,* by Mrs. Charles E. Cowman. My friend Mary Ellen had found it the day she took the framed Serenity Prayer back to the funeral home for me.

While trying to arrange the prayer stitchwork between the caskets, she felt something more was needed and had discovered *Streams in the Desert* at the local bookstore. While searching her billfold for money to pay for it, she idly explained to the clerk how she planned to use it.

"Here, please take it," the saleslady said, refusing payment. "My daughter was once in Mr. Smith's band. She loved him. Please let me make this a gift to him."

Each day the truths of the little book became more precious to me. Mrs. Cowman had obviously suffered as deeply as I was suffering. Her words comforted my heart.

I also quickly discovered that most people felt a deep need to help or offer comfort, but they did not know what to do. Their standard response was, "Call me if you need anything." I knew I would never call.

On the other hand, when someone saw a need and filled it, I was grateful. Lib, Linda and JoAnn came one day and cleaned my house. They changed the sheets, scrubbed the bathroom and vacuumed. Our friend Tom fixed the screen door. People prepared and brought whole meals. Others washed the dishes. Dottie and Mary Ellen were faithful in making sure Tonya was cared for, took her bath and wore clean clothes. Often they spent the night to keep us from being alone.

Some people tried to offer spiritual Band-aids. They often quoted Scripture or patted my hand saying, "All things work together for good for those who love the Lord." *Did I not love God enough?* I wondered. *Is that why He took Sonny and Greg and left me?*

"It was God's plan," others said. I could not help questioning, *What kind of selfish monster would devise a plan with this kind of pain?* Not a loving God, I felt sure.

Still others would say, "He needed them more than you did." How could He need Sonny more than Tonya needed a daddy or I needed my husband?

I got most angry when some well-meaning person said, "Don't worry, you'll see them again."

You don't know that, I wanted to scream. *You can't know that. Besides I don't want them in heaven. I want them now. I want to feel Sonny's arms around me, kiss his lips and hear his voice. I want to watch my son grow up. I don't want them in heaven. I want them now.*

Furthermore, in Luke 20:34, 35, I discovered this: "Marriage is for people here on earth, but when those who are counted worthy of being raised from the dead get to heaven, they do not marry (TLB)." I already knew, even if there were a heaven, I would never again know Sonny the way I knew him as my husband. That relationship, the most precious one I had ever known, was gone forever.

The people who comforted me most were those who just listened or talked with me about their special memories of Sonny and Greg. I appreciated those who were not afraid to say their names. I was grateful for those who did not feel they had to offer an answer. The comfort of loved ones, however, did not begin to ease the depth of my sorrow and sense of loss.

One day I was wandering aimlessly through the house, lost in my strange new world. A crumpled piece of yellow paper, lying on the green carpet in the living room, caught my eye. I recognized it from the note pad Tonya had scribbled on during the long bus ride to and from Florida.

I stooped down, picked it up and as I read it, a shiver inched up my spine. It said:

> *Dear Donna,*
>
> *Please don't worry about me. I am fine. I have to take care of my mommy.*
>
> > *Love,*
> >
> > *Tonya*

I stared at the crumpled note written in my daughter's sprawling, third-grade handwriting. I remembered how she had hovered over me since the accident, bringing me coffee, studying my face, holding my hand. I had never fully realized what might have been going through her mind.

Outwardly she had appeared not to comprehend what the deaths meant. I watched her playing with her friends just as she always had. She giggled, laughed and interacted normally with the stream of visitors pouring in and out of the house. Now I saw a clear picture of a little girl trying desperately to protect and care for all she had left.

I knew my growing time had come. Tonya deserved a mother. A sane, clear-thinking, caring, loving mother on whom she could depend. A mother who would be there even if the whole world shattered around her. I knew I had to be that mother.

I also knew I had to put her emotional and physical needs before my own. Whatever decisions I faced, she would have to be my first consideration. I never wanted her to feel different or deprived. I had to hold fast to the principles of love and discipline Sonny and I believed in. I had to create a home filled with love and trust. I wanted to bring her up in a way that would make Sonny and Greg proud of us both.

Stooped in the middle of my living room floor, holding the piece of crumpled yellow paper, I silently determined that Tonya would come out of this tragedy a strong and healthy child. I would be the best mother

I knew how to be. I would give my little girl the best life I knew how. Together we would not only survive, we would survive as healthy and whole individuals.

Without realizing it, I had also given myself a reason to go on living.

CHAPTER TEN

Lonely Nights

B Y the end of January, the periodic snowstorms finally quieted. Once again the yellow school buses lumbered along the mountain roads, picking up children who lived in the hollows and coves. I was grateful for the month off, but I knew it was time to return to my teaching job. I transferred Tonya from Hillandale to Dana Elementary School, so we could be together.

The night before school reopened, Neil Rogers, my principal; his wife, Elizabeth; and several co-workers from Dana brought supper and assured me of their support as I returned to the classroom. My co-teacher, Ann Banta, twenty-four years old and single, cooked a roast. "Now, Becky, that is real love," she said with a laugh. "I don't even cook for myself!"

Ann was especially dear to me. She was model-thin, had long blonde hair, and was gorgeous. She had been reared by her divorced mother in a high-rise apartment on the Gold Coast of Chicago, quite a contrast to my upbringing on the farm.

Despite the differences in our backgrounds, we shared the same values. We had both discovered early that life is what you make it. You do have the power to change your attitude and your circumstances. You can make life work for you, or you can whine because it is sometimes unfair.

Ann was a doer, not a whiner. In her, I saw it was possible for me to rear a happy, well-adjusted daughter alone. When I returned to the classroom, she became my inspiration, best friend and ally.

Every morning I took great care to be as neatly groomed as possible before I left for work. I felt compelled to look normal on the outside, so people would not suspect and be repulsed by the raw, bleeding mess on the inside. Like springs in a wind-up alarm clock, my nerves were wound so tightly I feared I might fly apart and spill out my insides for everyone to see.

Ann seemed to understand and shared my pain. She listened when I needed to talk about Sonny and Greg. She allowed me to cry and often cried with me. If she saw me struggling in the classroom, she would quietly take charge of the children and give me time to corral my runaway emotions.

Every day I struggled to keep a tight rein on my feelings, especially in front of the children. The needs of twenty-six five-year-olds demanded my constant, undivided attention. I knew I could not fail in my obligation and responsibility to them. They also gave me a reason to push my grief deeper inside.

Many times I felt life was utterly hopeless. It was then that I reminded myself of little Tonya; her very life depended on me. I had to get up in the morning and go on living for her sake, if for no other reason. I worried about her constantly. It was hard enough to change schools, make

94

new friends and adjust to a new teacher. But to make those adjustments while trying to cope with the loss of her father and brother was more than any child should have to bear.

On my way to the teachers' lounge, I often detoured by her room to catch a glimpse of her in her classroom. At recess I would search for her auburn hair and watch as she interacted with other children. I continually listened for clues of what she was thinking and tried to stay alert to her moods. I studied her facial expressions for signs of what she was feeling. She and I talked often about Sonny and Greg. We laughed about the good times and cried when we felt like it.

Before I knew it, Valentine's Day arrived. It was the anniversary of my first date with Sonny. We were in college and had ridden the church bus to a sweetheart banquet at the First Baptist Church in Rome, Georgia. I remember how stunning I felt in my white-lace dress with a hot-pink cummerbund. Sonny had given me a single, long-stemmed red rose, which became our symbol of love. This year, however, I knew there would be no valentine rose.

After lunch the children and I were working at the art table, making valentines for their mommies, when a knock sounded at the door. Ann opened it to find a florist deliveryman. He was carrying a vase of long-stemmed red roses. "These are for Mrs. Smith," he said.

"For me?" I exclaimed. "Who in the world would send me roses?"

Eagerly I tore open the envelope. The card read:

> *Mrs. Smith, Thinking of you today.*
> *We love you,*
> *Raymond and Clifford.*

Tears filled my eyes. Raymond and Clifford were two seniors from Sonny's band. They could not have known my sentimental attachment to Valentine's Day or long-stemmed red roses. At that moment, they became Sonny's arms around me. Through them, God gifted me with a precious surprise. Sadly, though, I did not recognize it was from Him.

As the cold February days dragged by, I discovered the reality of the truism: When one thing goes wrong, everything goes wrong. A wheel had fallen off my Volkswagen, and the motor on the washing machine died. I bought a new washing machine. Then the car brakes had to be replaced. Three weeks later, the clutch malfunctioned. By my birthday, on February 26, the turmoil inside me made me feel like an aged, worn-out woman instead of thirty-five. Every part of my body ached.

Going home after school each afternoon became increasingly painful. The house was empty and cold like death. I began escaping to the malls of the surrounding towns. They were warm and teemed with life. I found the hustle and bustle comforting.

One blustery afternoon in early March, Tonya and I were eating supper at the S & W Cafeteria. On our way home, just as we turned onto the Interstate 40, steam started boiling from underneath the car's hood. I screeched to a halt on the side of the road. "Hop out, quick, Tonya," I said frantically. "The car might blow up."

We ran a few yards down the road and waited. When nothing happened, we slowly inched back to the car, got in and waited for someone to stop and help. After a while, Tonya began to cry. She was cold and scared. Her crying agitated me.

"Come on, honey," I said. "Button your coat and put on your gloves. We'll walk for help."

We locked the doors and started walking. Cars whizzed by, blasting us with frigid air. After about a mile, Tonya's little face appeared blistered from the wind. Her teeth chattered uncontrollably.

"Mama, why don't we wait till the car cools off and then we can drive it to a service station?" she asked innocently.

I could not believe my stupidity. The thought had not occurred to me. *Becky, you are really losing your mind,* I chided myself as we trudged back to the car and waited until it was cool enough to drive. We puttered to a service station at the next exit. The car could not be fixed until the next day, so I called Johnnie and Pat Snyder, friends in Hendersonville. Johnnie came to pick us up. Later that night when Howard and Kat called, I told them about the car.

"Becky, we can't be down here worrying about you and Tonya getting stranded up there. You have to buy a new car," Howard said emphatically.

Buy a car? The only thing I knew about a car was that it took gas to run. After our conversation, I tried to educate myself about the best car to buy. I read consumer reports and articles. Talking with Sonny's friends proved to be a serious mistake; they all liked a different brand or model. Their suggestions only confused me more.

Finally Howard and I worked out an agreement. Each time I planned to talk with a dealer, he would wait by the phone in Florida. I would call him from the showroom, and he would talk to the salesman. After they finished, Howard would tell me whether I was getting a fair deal. Together we went through dealerships in Hendersonville, Asheville, and Brevard.

One day I asked Dottie's husband, Ted, to go with me to Boyd Pontiac in Hendersonville, the dealership where Sonny usually traded. The salesman knew Sonny, and I guess for that reason made a generous offer on my Volkswagen toward the trade-in on a new Pontiac Grand Prix. It was twice the amount anyone else had offered for my old car.

"May I think about it overnight?" I asked.

Poor Ted just shook his head. As we drove off the lot, he said, "I wouldn't leave here without buying that car at that price. You'll never get a better deal."

The next day I negotiated a trade and drove away in a beautiful, Carolina Blue Pontiac. Instead of new-car euphoria, I felt only relief.

Buying a car would have been difficult at any time, but having to buy one while I was in such emotional turmoil was a terrorizing experience.

Not long after I bought the car, a letter arrived from the Internal Revenue Service informing me that Sonny and I had been selected for a tax audit. They needed documents, proof of deductions and canceled checks. I did not know where to begin. Sonny had always taken care of our finances.

After many anxious hours, I was finally able to pull together all the information they requested. I mailed it and waited. Before long, I received a summons for a hearing in Asheville. I was frightened; a summons sounded threatening. I called the agent, whose name appeared on the letter, and explained about Sonny's death.

Then I said, "I'll be glad to come, but I don't have any additional information I can give you. If Sonny made a mistake, it was an honest mistake. If we owe additional taxes, then I'll just have to pay them."

The agent was courteous and pleasant. A few days later, I received a letter saying the audit had been satisfied, and no taxes or penalties would be imposed. I breathed a sigh of relief. Once again I learned how important it was for me or any woman to understand money management, family finances, taxes and fiscal accountability.

At the time of the airplane accident, I had been serving my second term as president of Hendersonville's Business and Professional Womens' Club. With the help of Betty McAllister, my dear friend and vice president, I continued to serve. The responsibility once again forced me to focus on something other than my grief. It also gave me another reason to push my grief a little deeper. I did not know a volcano was slowly building inside me.

Strange new fears began creeping into my life, especially at night. We had a basement in our house, and I worried constantly someone might break in through the downstairs door and harm Tonya or me. Anyone who read the newspaper in our small town knew about the accident and realized we were alone.

My growing fear magnified every sound—the wind blowing in the branches of the pine trees outside my bedroom window, the furnace starting to heat, hot water running through the pipes, a car easing slowly down the road. Lying in bed in the darkness, I heard them all. Many times a night, I planned how Tonya and I would escape through the bedroom window.

Unnerving calls and letters from strange men added to my fears. Immediately after the accident, letters began arriving from a man in Atlanta who said we had been in college together. I had no recollection of him. Every day for a week, I received long, intensely personal letters. One Sunday afternoon, he called.

"Did you get my letters, Becky?" he asked.

Anger surged through me like wildfire. "Yes, I did!" I exploded. "And let me tell you, I certainly do not appreciate this. My husband has just died, and I do not welcome your attention." I never heard from the man again.

Late one night another man called to invite me to join the local chapter of Parents Without Partners. Still another stranger called to express sympathy and wondered what he might do to help me. I could not believe such boldness. I also realized such a person might see nothing wrong with showing up at my door one day. I struggled not to let Tonya see how fearful I was becoming.

Wanting to show their love and concern, the students of East High had given us some money. I used part of it to buy a frisky Lhasa apso puppy. The Lhasa breed were often used as watch dogs, and I felt safer having him around. But he was ill-tempered and resisted being housebroken, so we finally had to give him away.

I toyed with the idea of bringing Greg's dog, Fonzie, home from

Mama's house, but I just could not do it. She had kept him while we went to Florida. I felt he was something of Greg's she could have and love. My heart ached for Mama and Daddy. I knew they grieved deeply. Sonny had been a son to them. Greg was their delight.

Greg and Tonya had loved Mama and Daddy and looked forward to spending time on the farm with them. The children loved to snuggle under layers of handmade quilts on a cold winter's night and listen to Mama tell mountain folklore stories. During the summer, Mama would stake out the best fishing spot at the pond and also let them help her feed the ducks. Sometimes she even pretended not to see while they chased her chickens.

Daddy often took them exploring across Pinnacle Mountain in the back of his truck or let them play in the church while he mowed the grass at Mount Olivet's graveyard. Sister Tonya led the imaginary congregation in singing; Brother Greg did the preaching. Playing church had been one of their favorite activities.

One summer Daddy gave Greg and Tonya their own piglets to raise. Greg named his Arnold and decided to enter him in the annual Apple Festival Kiddie Parade. Daddy, Sonny and Greg built a cage and loaded Arnold onto a little red wagon. Greg made a sign that said, The World's Smallest Elephant. Dressed like an animal trainer, Greg pulled Arnold's wagon along the parade route. Amid a menagerie of costumed children, barking dogs, mewing cats and honking ducks, an oinking Arnold did not seem at all out of place.

Now I knew Mama and Daddy sat on the mountaintop alone with their memories. Two fresh graves nearby were constant reminders of what they had lost. Their pain was deep; I hurt for them.

Being a parent myself, I also realized the helplessness they felt at not being able to bear my pain. I knew they would take it all from me, if only they could. Strangely, however, I was incapable of sharing my grief with them. I tried desperately to hide the agony, fear and confusion churning inside me.

Late at night and in the wee hours of the morning when I was alone, I grieved. Early on, I discovered grief makes other people uncomfortable. They do not want to talk about it. They do not want you to talk about it. After a short period, they move on with their lives and expect you to do the same.

I could not seem to move on. Grief completely paralyzed me. My deep sense of loss for Sonny and Greg was overwhelming. Their deaths seemed so meaningless. I searched in vain for a reason that seemed fair, just or even understandable. I could find none. At night I would lie down, weary of the constant pain, determined to sleep. For a little while, I might doze then suddenly awaken. When the thoughts and pain crawling around in my head became so torturous, I could not fight any longer. I would get up, make a pot of coffee and sit at the kitchen table for the rest of the night.

Sometimes I would try to read the Bible or pray. Other times all I could do was moan their names over and over—Sonny, Greg, Sonny, Greg. I now understood pain so deep there were no words to express it.

In Romans 8:26, I found the passage that fit my feelings: ". . . the Spirit himself maketh intercession for us with groanings which cannot be uttered (KJV)." I was relieved He could understand my groaning.

Over and over, I cried, "Why, God? Why?" I pleaded with Him to make me understand. Often I screamed at Him. Sometimes I whimpered. All my pleadings and groanings, however, were met with silence. The heavens were shut tight. God seemed far away, almost nonexistent.

Much of my waking hours were spent thinking and wondering about eternity. Even though Dr. Weaver had warned me about reading certain materials on life after death, my need to know continued to be urgent.

I devoured numerous books on death, dying and grief.

I bought a notebook and began keeping notes on my readings. One of the first things I discovered was the difference between sudden grief and anticipatory grief.

Anticipatory grief occurs when a lingering illness takes someone we love. Grieving starts from the moment we are told our loved one will not live. We have time to give physical as well as verbal expression to our love. We have the opportunity to say the things we want to say to each other.

Medical experts seem to agree that anticipatory grief has five stages: shock and denial, rage and anger, bargaining, depression, and acceptance. These stages vary in intensity and length, but sudden grief appears to have more of these stages. Anticipatory and sudden grief start with shock and denial. But numbing, not rage and anger, seems to be the second phase following a sudden death.

Sudden grief also robs its victims of the opportunity of saying goodbye. Too much is left unsaid; too many things are left undone. For that reason, grief is often more intense and lingers longer than if the death was anticipated.

The instant I heard Joan say there had been an airplane accident, shock ran through me like electric current. The typical psychological features of shock during the initial phase of a sudden death had surfaced: alarm, disbelief and panic. Unconsciously I had tried to keep the world sane by refusing to hear or believe the truth.

Then I experienced the second phase of sudden grief, a numbing sensation. It acted like a natural anesthetic and kept me from experiencing the total pain of my losses all at once. The numbness was why I was able to move through the funeral; I was on automatic pilot.

It was also interesting to learn about the actual physical changes that had taken place in my body that day. My blood pressure had lowered.

I found out why my skin had become so cold, my heart beat more rapid, and why I felt such an acute sense of terror. In the blink of an eye, an internal mental and emotional emergency alarm system went off inside me. All the meaningful linkups in my life had been jeopardized.

In addition, most experts cautioned me to give myself time to grieve. How could I do otherwise? I did not know how to stop the pain. Although I never felt angry with Sonny or Greg for dying, I felt intensely angry with God. He could have prevented their deaths. Sometimes I wanted to shake my fist at Him and scream at the top of my lungs, "What kind of God are you anyway?"

I also felt intensely lonely in my grief. I longed to have someone put his or her arms around me and say, "Becky, I really understand what you are feeling. I've been there."

I did not know anyone except Floy who had lost a husband and son at the same time, but talking on the phone to her did not offer the same comfort as talking face to face. Besides, we were both so lost in our own grief, we were not able to offer each other much comfort.

As I read and studied about coping with grief, my notebook continued to grow. I made notes about not making quick decisions concerning life-changing issues, such as moving, giving up my work, changing jobs or rushing too soon into another marriage. To do so would add shock to shock. Most experts suggested putting all big decisions on hold for at least a year to eighteen months.

Even though I filled my head and notebook with information about grief, I never found what I wanted most—peace for my hurting heart or tortured mind.

Lula Mae Briggs, my spiritual mom, continually urged me, "Becky, it's okay to read books, but they don't take the place of Scripture. Read your Bible. Study it. You'll find all the answers you need."

I tried to follow her advice but found myself even questioning the validity of the Bible.

One day a greeting card arrived from my friend Casey Bragdon. It contained a story by an unknown author, titled "Life is Eternal." It gave me a startlingly fresh insight into death.

> *I am standing upon the seashore. A ship at my side spreads her white sails to the morning breeze and starts for the blue ocean. She is an object of beauty and strength and I stand and watch her until at length she hangs like a speck of white cloud just where the sea and sky come down to mingle with each other. Then someone at my side says: "There! She's gone."*
>
> *Gone where? Gone from my sight—that is all. She is just as large in mast and hull and spar as she was when she left my side, and just as able to bear her load of living freight to the place of destination. Her diminished size is in me, not in her; and just at the moment when someone at my side says, "There! She's gone," there are other eyes watching her coming and other voices ready to take up the glad shout, "There she comes!"*

Could I believe that Sonny and Greg were just the same as they always were, just somewhere beyond my sight? Could it be they were still as real as they ever were? Oh, God, how I wanted to believe it to be true!

As a little girl, I had often heard John 14:2, 3 quoted at funerals: "In my Father's house are many mansions: if *it were* not *so,* I would have told you. I go to prepare a place for you. And if I go and prepare a place for you, I will come again, and receive you unto myself; that where I am, *there* ye may be also (KJV)."

It had always been easy for me to say I believed in heaven and hell because it never really mattered to me then. Now it mattered desperately.

I also read in 1 Corinthians 13:12, "For now we see through a glass, darkly; but then face to face: now I know in part; but then shall I know even as also I am known (KJV)."

Did that mean I would know Sonny in heaven as I knew him here on earth? Would he look the same? Would Greg still be twelve years old, or do we age in heaven? Would they know me? What kind of relationship would we have? Could any relationship ever match the joy of being husband and wife?

I read another passage in John, promising that even though we die we will live again; we will be given eternal life if we believe in Christ.

Do you believe this, Becky? I asked myself over and over. *What if we are just fooling ourselves?* I reasoned. *What if we just want to believe, and when we come to the end of life discover it is all a farce? What if Jesus' birth, death and resurrection were merely concocted by man?*

I forced myself to think deeply about these things. I had to know the truth.

Many times a day I passed the Serenity Prayer hanging in my hall and mouthed its words. I knew I could not change Sonny's and Greg's deaths. What I could do was change myself, my thinking, my habits. I had to learn to adapt to life without them. I struggled every day to make those changes.

By the time the Easter season arrived, four painful months had passed since the accident. My five-year-olds at school were full of excitement as they anticipated the arrival of the Easter Bunny. While we waited for the room mothers to hide the eggs on the playground for the big hunt, I sat in my rocking chair with a cup of coffee in my hand. The children clustered around my feet, chattering excitedly.

Kimberly asked, "Mrs. Smith, what's in that cup?"

"It's coffee."

"I like coffee," Billy said.

"Oh, Billy, I hope your mother doesn't let you drink coffee."

"Well, you drink it," he responded.

"Yeah, but I'm all grown up. I'm an old married woman."

"Oh, no, you're not," said Billy, shaking his head.

Not married? The thought rushed through my brain like a hurricane. "Well, yes, I am, honey. See my rings," I said, quickly pointing to my finger.

"No, you're not," Billy said again emphatically. "Your husband was killed. I read it in the newspaper."

"Ah, you can't read!" piped up Michael, giving him a poke in the stomach.

Their innocence was precious, but I felt as if someone had plunged a knife directly into my heart. I was not married! My husband was dead. *I am married,* I thought angrily. *I'll always be married.*

Even as I inwardly screamed denial, the impact of Billy's words seared my heart. No matter how I tried to deny it, my husband was dead. I was now single. A widow. Once again, I felt the familiar pain. Sorrow crashed over me like angry whitecapped waves each time reality flooded into my thoughts. Grief stormed through me with more frequency and force. Wave after pounding wave seemed to carry me deeper into the dark, murky waters of grief. I felt as if I were drowning.

CHAPTER ELEVEN

The Lady Slippers Bloom

L IKE *a mother tenderly covering her sick child with a soft blanket, spring came gently to the mountains. As the days* grew warmer, I realized it was time to begin thinking about the money contributed by the community to a memorial fund for Sonny and Greg. I discussed the matter with Sue Buttner and the band seniors. We decided to establish the Marion O. Smith Memorial Music Award at East High and the Marion Gregory Smith Memorial Art Award at Flat Rock Junior High.

The music award was to be a trophy to be given to a senior band member. His or her peers would vote for the one person who most exemplified the qualities Sonny felt were important in a band member: dependability, enthusiasm, loyalty and a willingness to work.

Greg's award would be a trophy, too. It would be given to the most promising art student selected by the art teacher at Flat Rock Junior

High. Sonny's oldest brother, Paul, owned a trophy business, so we commissioned him to design the trophies.

As the days grew warmer, yellow daffodils blossomed and spring fever attacked the schoolchildren. Their noise level and energy rose like sap in the trees. Their concentration soared out the window like a bird in flight.

One warm day in May, diminutive Sam Jones and I were sitting at a work table in back of the classroom. Sam was struggling to distinguish the differences in objects pictured on a work sheet, an important pre-reading skill he usually enjoyed. This day, however, the distractions were too many for him.

A bluebird on the porch railing chirped through the open door. A slight breeze ruffled the window curtains. Some children were playing in the housekeeping center; others were building a city with the wooden blocks. Catherine and Beth were measuring water at the water table. Sam wanted to be anywhere but with me. He fidgeted and poked the air with his pencil.

"What do you see, Sam?" I asked impatiently.

Sensing my frustration, he leaned back in his chair and flashed a big, I-dare-you-not-to-love-me, grin.

"Come on, Sam. You've got to finish this before you can go to recess," I pleaded, avoiding his big blue eyes.

Obediently, Sam leaned down and pored over the work sheet of insects, straining to find the one that was different.

"Look here, Sam. Look here," I finally said, jabbing my finger up and down on the correct one.

Little Sam looked down again, then up at me. His big blue eyes sparkled mischievously as he broke into a huge clown-like smile, revealing two missing front teeth.

"Well," he said slowly in pure mountain brogue, "he's a cute little ol' booger, ain't he?"

I burst out laughing. Sam laughed, too. For the first time since the accident, I laughed. Deep, belly-wrenching laughter. I laughed and laughed hysterically.

Ann came running. "Becky, what's going on?"

Suddenly the laughter turned to tears. I started to sob as Ann quickly ushered the children outside. Laying my head down, I wept uncontrollably as all the emotions I had been stuffing inside for months came pouring out. I cried until I could cry no more. Grief was like quicksand, always shifting.

As the spring days drifted by, a compelling need surfaced inside me. I became obsessed with knowing why the airplane had crashed. Mike Corbett secured a copy of the Federal Aviation Administration's investigative report for me. Somehow I needed to fill in the missing pieces.

After lunch on Mother's Day, Tonya and I drove to Winkler Aviation, a small private airport near our home. I hoped someone might be able to explain the dynamics of how a plane flies or what causes one to crash.

The airport held a lot of memories for me. Sonny, Greg, Tonya and I had sometimes taken short pleasure trips around the city when special promotions were offered. Sonny loved flying and was always fascinated with airplanes.

After we parked the car, we went straight to the airport office, hurrying past the small airplanes resting on the runway. A black-haired man in blue coveralls walked out to meet us.

"Can I help you, ma'am?" he asked pleasantly.

"I'd like to see Mr. Winkler, if I may," I replied.

"He's not here right now. I'd be glad to help if I can."

"No," I mumbled, trying to hide my disappointment. "I just wanted to ask him some questions."

As I turned to leave, the man startled me by asking, "You're Mrs. Smith, aren't you?"

"Well, yes," I replied.

"Mrs. Smith," he said, "I'm Mr. Duncan. I have worked at this airport for years. I know about the accident that killed your husband and son. I might be able to answer your questions."

"Oh, Mr. Duncan, I was never able to look at the airplane. Now I need to know what happened."

"Mrs. Smith, my daughter was one of Mr. Smith's students. She loved him. After the accident, I wanted to know what happened, so I flew to Florida and examined the wreckage. I think I can tell you what you want to know.

"The way I understand it," he explained, "they were flying low to take pictures over the house. As they tried to gain altitude, they couldn't generate enough speed or power to pull out of it. The engines stalled, and the plane nosedived into the ground. It was like hitting a brick wall at 180 miles per hour."

"Mr. Duncan, did Greg know what was happening?" I asked.

"No, ma'am, I don't believe so. It was all over in about five seconds."

"Did they suffer?"

"I don't think they could have. The impact was so great; they all died instantly. Their bodies couldn't take the trauma."

My emotions were screaming, *No, I don't want to hear this.* But my mind was saying, *They didn't suffer. My little Greg didn't suffer. He did not lay in the wreckage half conscious and racked with pain. He took one breath here and the next one in eternity.* I wept openly as I listened.

"Mr. Duncan, thank you for your time. You've helped me tremendously," I said, shaking his hand.

"We loved Mr. Smith," he said. "We appreciated what he meant to our daughter and what he did for our school and community, Mrs.

Smith. We grieve, too."

In the days following our conversation, I found myself repeatedly saying, "Thank you, God, that they didn't suffer. Thank you, thank you."

At last I had one thing in my life for which I could be thankful. I felt genuine gratitude their deaths were pain free. I was also grateful to God for placing Mr. Duncan at the airport to answer my questions.

For the first time since the accident, I started to feel a sense of God's presence in my life. A glimmer of hope flickered faintly in my heart. It was May, time for the lady slippers to bloom.

CHAPTER TWELVE

A New Friend

I was scheduled to present the Marion O. Smith Memorial Music Award at East High before school was dismissed in June. My courage wavered every time I thought about standing in front of the students to say goodbye. Inwardly I rebelled at the thought that East High would no longer be a part of my life. For ten years I had been Sonny's partner in his work. I had not only lost Sonny and Greg, I had really lost my whole way of life.

When I drove to the school on Awards Day, my heart fluttered with fear. I had not been to the high school since that dreadful day following the funeral. Easing into the parking lot beside the band room, I sat for a moment trying to calm my jitters. A rap sounded on the window. It was Sue Buttner; she had come to help me make it through the ceremony.

Sue and I waited backstage of the auditorium as other honors were awarded. Finally it was time for what I considered to be the most important award of the day. My breath came in short stabs of pain.

Charles Johnston, president of the Student Council and also a band member, introduced me, "Now, here to present the first Marion O. Smith Memorial Music Award is his widow, Mrs. Becky Smith."

As I strode onto the stage, the students stood and spontaneously erupted into applause. When they sat down and the applause died, I tried to speak, but no words would come. Only the sound of our sobs echoed in the hollow stillness of the giant auditorium. We wept together for what had been taken from us.

Helplessly, I turned to Charles. He gave me a warm hug. Sue's hand on my back gave me strength. With as much courage as I could scoop from within, I thanked the students and teachers for their influence. I thanked the band for surrounding us with their love. Finally I read the selections for the music award. Eddie Watkins and Doug Buttner, captain and co-captain of the last Marion Smith band at East High, had been voted to receive the award. I felt pride in their selection; they had been outstanding leaders.

As soon as I finished my presentation, I hurried out the back door to my car. Another important tie in my life had just been severed. I felt sick and wanted to vomit. With that task completed, I could hardly wait for school to be out. I needed to take care of myself. I was emotionally exhausted.

For vacation, Tonya wanted to go camping at Myrtle Beach, South Carolina, just as we had always done as a family. "Aunt Dot and Uncle Ted are going to stay three weeks. Can we go with them?" she begged. "Please, Mama, please."

I knew I needed to make life as normal as possible for her, even vacation time, but I was finding it exhausting to be both mother and father to her. Secretly I wondered if there was enough of me to do it all.

Ted and Dottie thought it was a wonderful idea, so after the last teachers' work day, we packed our camping gear and followed them to Myrtle Beach.

I welcomed the change in environment. For the past five-and-a-half months, I had often felt like a caged animal in an experimental medical lab. I would dart one way, then another, trying to find a place to hide, but there was no safe shelter. I was trapped in a maze of pain. Every time I got too near the bars, an unseen enemy jabbed me with a knife.

Reality was my unseen enemy as it continued to invade my waking hours. The slashes became more penetrating, the wounds deeper. Shock had somewhat protected me, allowing me to function. Now an intense physical pain accompanied frequent flashes of memory and the reality of my losses.

The moment Tonya and I drove into Lakewood Campground, I realized our coming was a mistake. This was a place for whole families; ours had been cut in half. On the way in, we circled a pond near the campground store. Immediately my eyes were drawn to a redheaded boy fishing from the bank. He reminded me of Greg. The sight of him stabbed my insides.

Across the lake, a family of four drifted leisurely by in a paddle boat. We drove past happy children on bicycles and three giggling teenage girls in a surrey with a fringe on top. Memories of our happy times together as a family clamored in my brain.

By nightfall, Ted, Dottie and I had stationed their camper and erected my tent on an adjoining site. Tonya begged to spend the night in the camper. As I snuggled down alone in my sleeping bag, I was finally able to release the pent-up tears I had held in check for so long. I wept for Sonny and Greg. I still could not understand why they had to die. I cried because I had lost God somewhere. I did not know where He was or who He was anymore. I felt He had betrayed me.

I wept for little Tonya, so sweet and innocent. I cried for myself, too. The pain inside was killing me, and I did not know how to make it stop. Instead of getting better, it was getting worse. Life was not worth living anymore. I longed to die, too. I cried until, lulled by the incessant waves nearby, I finally fell asleep.

I awoke the next morning determined to stay steady. But all around me, I watched daddies playing in the ocean; daughters riding on their shoulders; families building sand castles; and bikini-clad teenagers riding the white-capped waves. From sunup to sundown, the beach throbbed with activity.

Physically, I joined in the play with Ted, Dottie and the children as best I could. We rode the waves, played putt-putt golf and soaked in the sun. Even in the midst of our play, however, I felt more alone than I had ever felt in my life.

I often got up early and strolled along the beach, watching the sun rise, pleading with God for rest from the constant pain. I found the contradictions in my own thinking quite odd. I felt so isolated from Him, yet I knew He was the only hope I had. Only He had the power to change my life or relieve the pain.

Day after day, Ted and Dottie continued to be my perfect example of sacrificial giving and unselfish love. They had been devoted to Tonya and me since the accident. Dottie often cooked our meals, cleaned the house, washed and even ironed our clothes. Ted had helped me with the car, business matters and provided a strong arm for us to lean on. They had taken us places with their family and given us a home away from home. They prayed with us and for us. I was grateful for their steadfastness and love.

On our last Sunday morning at the campground, I heard gospel music drifting from the pavilion and impulsively decided to attend the worship service. Quickly slipping into a clean pair of white shorts and blue top,

I tied a turban around my hair and hurried toward the music. I found a seat on the back row of the rough-hewn log benches.

When the chaplain introduced the speaker, he said, "Folks, our guest today is Harold Morris. Harold was released from prison just three months ago, and today he wants to share with you a story of how he came to be there, how he came to know Jesus, and what God has done in his life."

Harold Morris appeared to be in his late thirties or early forties; he was clean-cut and neatly groomed in his navy suit. Since he had on long sleeves, I could not see his arms. *All convicts have tattoos,* I thought.

"Folks," he began, "I appreciate the opportunity to be with you today and tell you about my Lord and Savior, Jesus Christ. I wouldn't be here if it were not for Him."

Harold Morris immediately plunged into stories of being reared in nearby Georgetown, South Carolina. He told of growing up to become an all-state athlete in three sports. He rejected numerous college scholarship offers, choosing instead to marry his high school sweetheart and get a job. Later realizing the value of a degree, he enrolled at Guilford College in North Carolina.

During his senior year, he began to drink, do drugs and have extramarital affairs. This led to a divorce and eventually to prison after he was convicted of armed robbery and murder. "I did not commit the crimes for which I was charged and convicted," he declared.

Sure, I thought. *They all say that.*

Nevertheless, Harold continued to tell how he and two men he met in a night club traveled to Atlanta, where they partied for a week. Just before returning home, the two men decided to rob a supermarket. A bystander pulled a pistol during the robbery, and they shot him. Running back to where Harold was waiting, they jumped in the car and yelled, "Drive! Drive! We shot a man!"

While Harold was driving the getaway car, he asked them, "Did you kill him?"

"Naw, he was still standing. He'll live," they said.

When the trio arrived back in North Carolina, they parted ways. Harold did not see them again until a year later when he was arrested and charged with armed robbery and murder. The two men appeared as state's evidence, swearing it was he who had actually committed the crime.

"Don't feel sorry for me," Harold Morris said. "I got what I deserved. You see, I associated with the wrong kind of people, and I became like them.

"For five years, I sat in a lonely prison cell. No one knew where I was. I was too ashamed to even let my family know. I never wrote a letter, and I never received one. One day someone saw my picture in an old *True Detective* magazine in a beauty shop in Georgetown and notified my family. My brother Carl found me in the Georgia State Prison.

"Later, an old high school classmate who had been shot in the Vietnam War visited me and told me how God loved me and died for my sins. He gave me a Bible, and his wife wrote down some Scriptures for me to read. That night I thumbed through the Bible and found the verses. For hours I cried and reread the Scriptures. Then I fell on my knees in that filthy, roach-infested cell and cried out to Jesus, admitting my sin and begging His forgiveness. God heard the cry of my heart and cleansed my sin, filling me with joy and peace as I'd never known."

Harold Morris continued to tell us of his remaining years in prison and finally how he had been paroled. "God freed me," he said, "and I promised Him I'd spend the rest of my life telling others about Him, perhaps helping them avoid the mistakes I've made."

Harold spoke of God with great tenderness, as if he knew Him personally. After all this man's terrible experiences, he still believed in God.

When the service was over, I could not move. I gripped the log bench so hard my hands hurt. This man had something I wanted, faith and a personal relationship with a living God. Harold had suffered just as I was suffering. He knew about pain. Maybe he could help me find the God I had lost.

People thronged around Harold. Many were making first-time commitments to Christ; others were rededicating their lives. I hung back, debating whether I should just walk away. Suddenly Harold looked at me. Our eyes met. I do not know if he saw my pain, but he left the crowd and made his way toward me.

"Ma'am, can I help you?" he asked.

"How. . .how can you stand up there and talk about God. . .and how He's blessed you? How can you talk about faith after what you've been through?"

We walked to a nearby bench and sat down. "Ma'am, I don't know how to answer that. But if you'd like, I'd be glad to listen if you need to talk."

I spilled out the story of the accident. Then Harold said, "Are you camping here?"

"Yes," I nodded.

"Can you come back tomorrow so we can talk some more? I'll meet you in the chaplain's office at eleven o'clock."

"Okay," I agreed, and we parted with a handshake.

The rest of the day I chided myself for being so stupid. Harold Morris did not care about me. He did not know more about God than I did. I was just going to have to find Him myself. I had Him once; I could find Him again. It was simply a matter of getting control of my mind and emotions. As soon as I could do that, God would reappear in my life.

The next morning, I was determined to forget about my conversation with Harold Morris. After breakfast, Dottie and I watched our girls conduct a Miss America pageant. They paraded through the tent flaps with towels wrapped around their heads, pretending the towels were long hair. They pranced, modeled make-believe evening gowns and answered interview questions.

I tried to push thoughts of Harold Morris aside, but his message kept ringing in my ears. "God really does love you, Becky. If He cares about an ex-convict like me, surely He cares about you."

The closer the time inched to eleven o'clock, the more scared I became. *He's not going to be there,* I told myself. *He can't help you anyway. You're nothing to him. Don't go.*

At that moment, I decided once and for all I would not go. At the same time, Tonya announced, "And our new Miss North Carolina is"—then she paused for effect—"Miss Crystal Leighanne Beddingfield. Take the runway, Crystal."

After Crysti returned, Tonya continued. "And now presenting your new Miss South Carolina, Andrea Tiffani Beddingfield. Meet your subjects, Miss South Carolina."

After Tiffi's victory stroll, Tonya continued, "And now presenting, for the first time, our new Miss America." She gave a drum roll and then said, "Tonya Lynette Smith." Crysti and Tiffi cheered obediently as she flung back her towel hair and strolled down the runway, waving to her imaginary subjects.

I watched in amusement, delighted with their ability to pretend. Remembering Pop Beddingfield's nickname for the girls made me smile. Tonya was Tangerine; Crysti was Twig; and Tiffi was Andrew. I wondered if the real Miss America would ever have such a nickname.

Glancing at my watch, I saw it was just seconds before eleven. *What if Harold Morris is waiting for me?* I wondered. I tied a scarf around my unkempt blonde hair, smeared on some pink lipstick and ran toward the pavilion.

You fool, I chided myself, dodging a Frisbee.

Suddenly between the trees, I spied the pavilion and then Harold Morris. He had kept his promise. I slowed to a walk, trying to catch my breath.

Harold and I went into the chaplain's office, sat down and began to talk. Mostly, I talked, and he listened. He did not have a magic solution, but he was firm in his conviction that God had a plan for my life, and that He loved me.

"I hope you don't mind me asking this, Becky. But I need to know if you've ever asked Jesus Christ into your life."

"Yes," I told him. "I grew up in the church, but I know for sure I was saved when I was fourteen, in the ninth grade. A group of college students came to my school and gave a dramatic presentation of the gospel. As they closed the program with prayer, I silently asked the Lord to come into my heart and be my Lord and Savior. I know I'm saved. I'm just not sure about anything else anymore.

"I can't understand or reconcile how a God who loves me could allow my family to be cut in half. Why did he let Sonny and Greg die so suddenly, so violently? Sonny had such a productive, meaningful life. Greg never had a chance. I don't understand how a loving God would allow Tonya to grow up without her daddy or inflict such pain on us both.

Harold, I really don't even want to go on living anymore. I wish I could just die," I said with a sob. "Sometimes I just want to kill myself and get it over with."

"I know," he said, patting my hand. "I've felt that way, too. But you can't do that. You've got too much to live for. Your little girl needs you. You have to go on. Just trust Him, Becky. He does have a plan for your life."

Finally, there was nothing left to say. We prayed together, then parted with a handshake. As I walked back to my campsite in the noonday sun, Harold drove by and tooted the horn. I waved goodbye.

For a moment, Harold Morris had touched my life. I was grateful. I wrote him a note, thanking him for his time and counsel and mailed it to the Orangeburg Boys Home, where he worked.

There was no way I could have known then how God planned to use this man in my life and Tonya's. Even though I had yet to recognize it, He was already beginning to unfold His plan for our lives.

CHAPTER THIRTEEN

Happy Anniversary

T HE next day Tonya and I left Myrtle Beach and drove to Florida to spend the remaining weeks of summer vacation with Granddaddy and Grandmother Smith. Kat and Howard's daughter, Cheryl, was getting married. Tonya was to be her flower girl. When we arrived, I was shocked to see the toll grief had taken on Granddaddy and Grandmother Smith. They had aged dramatically, heartbreakingly.

During our stay, I often caught glimpses of Granddaddy standing beside his workshop, staring at the open field where the plane had gone down. Occasionally I would hear him in the bedroom playing the tape of Sonny singing, "Jesus, we just want to thank You." Other times, he would simply burst out weeping. The heavy weight of grief seemed more than his seventy-seven-year-old shoulders could carry.

Grandmother had lost weight. Her eyes were sunken and hollow and circled with dark rings. She did not sleep well. At night, I often heard her quietly stirring around. Nonetheless, she continued to cook three full meals a day, cultivate her flowers, fill the freezer with fresh vegetables and take care of Granddaddy.

My admiration and love for them continued to grow as they taught me by example how to deal with grief but never give in to its immobilizing power. Grief was not unfamiliar to them. Twenty-nine years earlier, they had lost their ten-year-old daughter Peggy, when a drunk driver smashed into Granddaddy's truck.

We talked often and cried a lot together. Even through the tears, they always said, "Becky, you've got to be strong. We all do. We can't give in. We've got to keep going."

I knew they were right. What choice did we have? Committing suicide was the only escape I knew from the pain. Unless I was willing to do that, there was nothing to do but bear the sorrow until it subsided.

Cheryl's wedding was lovely. We all tried hard to put our grief aside and be happy. Her new husband, Skip, had just graduated from Florida State University and accepted his first job as a high school band director in Atlanta. I thought it ironic that Cheryl's life might parallel mine. She was eight years old when Sonny and I married and had always been my baby.

A week later, as Tonya and I prepared to leave Florida, Howard called and asked us to stop by. When we arrived, he handed me two white envelopes. Alachua County Health Department was printed on the upper left-hand corner. I knew they were the death certificates. For a long time I just held them, not sure I wanted to know what they said.

For eight months I had clung tenaciously to the belief Sonny and Greg died whole, not broken and torn. If this was not true, I did not want to know it. Nervously, I fingered the envelopes. The feelings I experienced in the funeral home came rushing back over me. Did I want to know?

Trembling, I finally tore open the one on top. I sucked in hard and began to read. Greg's certificate showed that he had died of cerebral lacerations and skull fractures. Other significant conditions included a fracture of the right femur bone.

Quickly I withdrew from the searing pain, shut out the thoughts and blocked out reality. My breath came in those familiar short, painful spasms.

Hurriedly I tore open the other envelope. Sonny's read the same. Both their right legs had been broken. *How could that have happened?* I wondered, stuffing the documents back into the envelope. I struggled to wipe away the mental images. *Think about it later, Becky. Stay steady,* I coaxed myself.

Tonya and I said goodbye to Kat and Howard, then we headed north. By the time we reached Interstate 75, I could breathe normally once more. The nine-hour trip home stretched before us. To pass the time, Tonya and I played billboard games, school and store. I bought diamond watches and Barbie dolls. She learned to make change.

Late in the afternoon, the majestic North Carolina mountains finally loomed into view. We had been gone most of the summer, and I could hardly wait to get home. My heart pounded with excitement as our little red brick house came into view. I hurried to unlock the door and rushed inside.

I headed straight for Greg's room. It was still just as he had left it. I picked up the picture of him holding his white pet rabbit. He smiled at me. I smiled back and gave him a kiss. He was still with me.

In my bedroom I opened Sonny's underwear drawer, took out a T-shirt and stroked my face with it, recalling the touch of his body. His smell, his presence still lingered. I could feel it. It was good to be home.

Later I was walking back down the hall twisting my engagement ring, when suddenly a sharp prong pricked my thumb. I looked down. My diamond was missing!

"Oh, no," I screamed aloud. "Not my diamond!"

Tonya came running.

"Oh, honey, help me find my diamond," I begged, feeling panicky.

Frantically I crawled around on my hands and knees, retracing my steps across the floor, but I didn't find it. Running for the vacuum cleaner, I found an old pair of pantyhose, cut them apart and jerked a piece of hose over the nozzle. Then I vacuumed the floor down the hall and into the bedrooms while Tonya searched the kitchen. I just could not lose my diamond. Sonny had worked so hard at night in a warehouse to buy it for me. Panic was rising and falling with each breath. I had to find my diamond. I felt as if I were going berserk.

"Mama, I found it!" she called, running to me. "Here it is!"

"Oh, thank God. Where was it?" I sobbed.

"On the kitchen floor by the suitcase."

Cradling the tiny jewel in the palm of my hand, my tears washed it clean. I could not stop crying. Suddenly I realized how out of control I had become. My emotional roller coaster was gaining speed. I did not know how much longer I would be able to hang on. I was losing the control I had struggled so long to maintain.

School started the following week. Tonya and I returned to Dana Elementary. She enrolled in fourth grade, and I began with a new class of kindergartners. Soon our life settled into a routine dictated by school. I had hoped the summer away from my responsibilities would give me time to better deal with my grief. Instead I found myself in worse shape than ever before. The cocoon of shock was completely gone. Reality was now my constant companion.

I finally knew in my heart what I had known with my intellect at the time of the accident—Sonny and Greg were never coming back. Death was real and forever. Life for me and Tonya would never be the same.

With these realizations came pain so constant and intense, it was agonizing.

Fall was band season. I stayed away from Hendersonville's annual Apple Festival Parade and high school football games to avoid seeing the band without Sonny. I just was not ready for the shock.

Memories of Sonny, however, would not leave me alone. I went to bed with them at night and woke up with them in the morning. They played games in my mind, popping in and out like children in a game of hide and seek. I found myself waking up, listening for Sonny singing in the shower. In the evening I waited anxiously for the whine of his truck engine and the sound of his footsteps.

Sometimes I would catch myself searching the road in back of the house, watching for Greg to come home from the lake. I passed Flat Rock Junior High every day and caught myself hungrily searching the grounds for just a glimpse of his little freckled face in the crowd.

One beautiful Saturday afternoon, Tonya and I picked up the mail at the Flat Rock Post Office and drove slowly toward home. A few yards from the post office, we passed Peace's Grocery, our tiny neighborhood store.

Suddenly I remembered the charge account Sonny had given Greg when he started junior high. He was free to use it for an afternoon Pepsi, an ice cream or a candy bar. It was Sonny's way of recognizing his son's independence as he neared the teen years.

"Honey, we'd better check with Mr. Peace about Greg's bill. I completely forgot about it," I said, circling back around.

Age had taken its toll on Peace's Grocery. The building was so old and tired it was not sure which way it wanted to fall, so it just stood. Clarence Peace, an elderly bachelor, inherited it from his parents. It had been in operation since I was a little girl. When Tonya and I stepped inside the store, it was dark and gloomy. The wooden planks groaned beneath our feet.

"Mr. Peace, I'm here to pay Greg's bill," I explained. "I'm sorry I haven't been here sooner, but I forgot about it."

"No problem, Mrs. Smith. Let me find it," Mr. Peace said, putting on his wire-rimmed glasses. He started to mumble under his breath and smack his lips, a habit I found irritating.

As the gray-haired man sifted through his files, I glanced around. Two uncovered light bulbs glowed overhead. An old-fashioned telephone booth with glass doors and a wooden seat stood in the corner. Dust covered rows of canned goods along the walls. A half-eaten hot dog and can of beans rested on the counter beside the cash register. Fresh mustard-colored stains on Mr. Peace's shirt told me I had interrupted his dinner.

"Here it is, Mrs. Smith," he said, handing me the ledger card.

I studied it carefully. Each purchase had been itemized and dated. Soft drinks, ice-cream sandwiches, bubble gum and candy bars. The total was two dollars and sixty-seven cents. My little Greg had managed well. I could just see him standing at the counter, selecting a candy bar from the glass case.

Fighting back the tears, I counted out the change to pay his bill. *I would give everything I own, even my own life, if only I could have the chance to buy my son just one more Pepsi,* I thought. It was the ordinary, everyday things I missed the most.

The following Wednesday night I was getting ready for choir practice when the phone rang.

"Hello, Becky," said a strange male voice. "This is Harold Morris. How are you doing?"

I was shocked. "Harold Morris? How did you get my phone number?" I knew I had not given it to him, and I was not sure I had ever told him Sonny's real name was Marion.

"Ex-cons have connections," he laughed. "Becky, I'm really concerned about you. Tell me how you're doing."

"I'm doing the best I know how right now, living one day at a time. I don't think beyond that. Sometimes I feel as if I'm in the ocean at Myrtle Beach, and the waves are tossing me around like a rag doll. When one turns me loose, another wave sweeps me up and carries me farther out to sea. I feel as if I'm fighting all the time just to keep from drowning. If I ever give up struggling, Harold, I'm afraid I'll sink to the bottom and never come up. I have to hang on."

We talked for a long time, then Harold said, "Becky, write down my phone number. I want you to call anytime, even if it's just to talk. Call collect. I'll be here for you."

As I laid the phone back in the cradle, I shook my head in disbelief. Harold had no reason to be interested in my welfare, yet he was. Once again, I failed to recognize the hand of God at work in my life. I did not know He was giving me a friend who would forever impact my faith and life.

In September, officials from two contests, which the East High band always participated in, called to say they wanted to honor Sonny at their upcoming festivals. They asked Tonya and me to be present. I agreed and thanked them for remembering him in such a meaningful way.

On the day of the first band festival, Tonya and I drove to Enka High School in Asheville. The East High band was scheduled to march in the late afternoon. I braced myself for the first sight of the familiar green-white-and-black uniforms. I caught myself wondering how my flag corps girls would look. I loved my girls.

Before the contest began, an announcer's voice boomed over the loudspeaker, "Today the Land of the Sky Festival is being dedicated to the memory of Marion O. Smith, deceased band director of East Henderson High School. Marion and his son, Greg, were killed in an airplane crash on December 27, 1977. Marion served East High for ten years. He was president of the Western North Carolina Band Directors Association at the time of his death. Today we honor his memory and welcome his widow, Mrs. Becky Smith, and his daughter, Tonya. Shall we pray?"

After a prayer of dedication, the first band took the field, and a long afternoon of competition began. The sight and sounds of the rhythmic drumbeats, swishing flags and tooting horns were so familiar, I was lulled into a fantasy that things were just as they had always been. I felt as though I were waiting in the stands while Sonny got his band ready to perform. Anticipation began to build for the magic moment when they would appear. Eagerly I searched the infield for them as band after band lined up for their performance.

Suddenly I spied green-and-white flags waving in the breeze. My heart skipped a beat. I waited breathlessly for the first sight of the band as it started down the bank—110 band members led by my Sonny. A lump lodged in my throat and my heart pounded. Suddenly they marched into view.

Something was horribly wrong. They were half their usual number. *What happened to the other band members?* I questioned. *Where is Sonny? Did a bus break down? Why are they lining up in the end zone as if nothing is wrong?*

The announcer introduced the band. *No, no we have to wait for the others,* I thought with panic. *Sonny is not there, but they are marching onto the field. Stop! Stop! Stop!* I cried to myself, but they kept right on marching.

Of course, I knew nothing was wrong. Yet everything was wrong. The whole world was wrong. "God, I hate you!" I cried aloud.

Instantly I recoiled in horror. What had I said? Embarrassed, I looked around at the puzzled expression of people sitting nearby. *They think*

I'm crazy. I am crazy. I am losing my mind.

"Let's go," I said to Tonya, grabbing her hand. We practically ran from the stadium.

Shortly after the band contest, I walked into the teachers' lounge one morning, having spent another sleepless night. The clock on the wall read nine-twenty.

"Please Lord," I prayed. "Just help me make it till ten-twenty." I felt I was struggling now, not just one day at a time but one hour at a time. Somehow I had to hold onto even a thin thread of emotional sanity.

The one friend who seemed to really know and understand was Harold Morris. We talked often. He let me pour out all my fears, frustrations and hurts. He was never shocked when I told him how hopeless life had become or how thoughts of suicide kept playing games in my head. One particular night he must have sensed how desperate I was.

"I'm coming to see you," he said. "Just hold on. I'll be there by noon tomorrow. We'll go on a picnic."

He came, and we spent the day in one of my favorite picnic spots high in the mountains of Pisgah National Forest. The cool breeze and the listening ear of my friend seemed to calm my spirits and help me regain some control of my runaway emotions. I told Harold about the band festival, my hurt and those awful words I screamed at God.

"That's okay," Harold said. "God knows you're hurting. He understands."

"Somehow I feel He does, but I'm so ashamed. I know if I'm to survive and for life to ever make sense again, God is the answer. I just don't know where He is or how to find Him."

"Becky, reading your Bible and praying is the only way you'll ever know Him," Harold said. "Burying yourself in His Word may not make much sense to you now, but it will. Just keep on doing that, and you'll start to see results in your life. I'll keep praying for you, Becky. It's going to get better one day, I promise."

We left the picnic grounds and drove home to pick up Tonya. She fell in love with Harold because he told her corny jokes. We both hugged him as he left.

The afternoon had been good for us. Harold seemed to bring the touch of a male presence to our lives and restored a little of our lost sense of security. I did not feel quite so vulnerable, so alone. I was grateful for my new friend.

September twentieth arrived. It was Sonny's and my fourteenth wedding anniversary. I had once again resumed my spring habit of not returning home until bedtime. Every afternoon Tonya and I were back on the road or in a mall somewhere. That afternoon we happened to stop at a clothing store in nearby Fletcher. Sonny and I had done some of our Christmas shopping together there.

As I wandered from the dress department through the lingerie, I suddenly spied a delicate pink negligee that Sonny and I had drooled over at Christmas. He had wanted so badly to buy it for me, but $79.95 was more than we could afford.

I picked up the filmy pink skirt of the gown. It floated through my fingers like silk. It was the color of cotton candy and felt just as light. I traced the pink lace on the top and fingered the tiny white pearl buttons, remembering the twinkle in Sonny's eyes as he touched the delicate softness. On a sudden impulse, I took it off the rack and hurried to the cash register. "Oh, that's one of the prettiest sets we've ever had," the saleslady said as I pulled out my checkbook.

"Yes, I know," I said. "My husband wanted to buy it for me at Christmas, but we couldn't afford it. He's dead now, but I'm buying it for him. Today's our anniversary." We both cried as I handed her the check.

That night when I got ready for bed, I took a long, hot bath. Drying off, I soothed my body with lotion, then dusted on body powder. I sprayed on my favorite cologne, then pulled the filmy, pink nightgown over my head. I fluffed up my hair and put on some pink lipstick. I put on the lace-covered robe and buttoned the delicate pearl buttons. Then I stood back and looked at myself in the mirror. I felt beautiful.

"Happy anniversary, sweetheart," I whispered. "I love you."

Somehow I knew Sonny was smiling.

CHAPTER FOURTEEN

Asleep in His Arms

AS the fall days drifted by, I felt myself getting weaker. My emotions were like a stormy ocean; they were becoming more turbulent by the hour. Incessant waves of grief were pounding the life out of me. My will to survive was almost gone.

When I lay down at night, the fear of someone breaking in to harm Tonya and me was ever present. I was still haunted by Sonny's empty place beside me. When I tried to sleep, visions of blood and twisted metal often invaded my dreams.

One night I woke up screaming as I saw the plane hurtling downward in my dreams. I could see Greg's eyes filled with terror when he cried out and grabbed for his daddy. For a moment, I was unable to move; my heart pounded violently. Perspiration bathed my body, and I could barely breathe.

Finally I threw back the covers and stumbled through the darkness to Greg's room. A tiny light streamed from his clock radio, casting shadows across his empty bed. I crumbled to the floor beside it and cried into his pillow. In utter desperation, I screamed aloud, "God, if You're there, and if You're real, You've got to help me. I can't go on like this."

Total darkness enveloped my soul as thoughts of suicide began crawling around inside my mind. I waited for God to show Himself to me. The silence, however, was broken only by the sound of my own sobs as the night disappeared into morning.

Not long after that frightful night, God did come to visit me in an unexpected time and place. He slipped quietly down beside me on the steps of my classroom and used a little boy named Mark to teach me about Himself.

Halloween was drawing near. The children's nervous energy was fueled by their excitement over Halloween. They jumped around like a herd of kangaroos.

To release some of their pent-up energy, Ann and I took them out for afternoon recess. Some children ran to the swings, others to the see-saws. Several boys raced for the towering oak tree to check on the warrior ants.

Suddenly shrill screams pierced the air. "Go away, Mark! Mrs. Smith, make Mark leave us alone. He's bothering us." I looked up to see Mark chasing several girls with a stick.

Mark was so tiny, I did not know if he had the strength to hurt them. Actually I was glad to see him interacting at any level. Mark was my puzzle and challenge. His frail body was spaghetti-thin, his brown eyes hauntingly blank. In the classroom, he usually sat on the floor, folded his bony knees together and stared at the carpet. The only way I could look into his eyes was to pull him to me and cup his face in my hands. Even then, he would not look directly at me.

The school nurse had told me that his parents were mentally handicapped and had almost let him starve to death when he was a baby. His mother would simply forget to feed him. The nurse marked his bottles with a magic marker and taught the mother to feed him by certain television programs. His little body still showed the effects of the neglect.

Mark became my special project. I was determined to discover the person hiding behind the mask of fright. I lavished him with love and attention and watched eagerly for any sign of progress.

"Mark, honey, the girls don't like you chasing them," I tried to explain, stooping down to put my arms around him. "Why don't you go help the boys under the tree? They're watching the ant army."

"Okay," he said and ran off to join them.

A few moments later, I heard it again. "Mrs. Smith, Mark's messing up our ants."

"Mark, come here," I said.

This time, he looked squarely at me and ran the other way, straight into the middle of a kickball game.

"Mark!" I said sternly, scooping him up in my arms when I finally caught him.

"Put me down!" he screamed, kicking his feet and flailing his arms. "Put me down!"

"Mark, stop it."

"Put me down," he howled. He continued to create such a scene, I took him away from the playground. He kicked and screamed as I carried him back to our building. The more he carried on, the tighter I held him.

"Mark, I am not going to turn you loose until you quit acting this way. Just calm down," I said softly.

I sat down on the steps of the building and clutched him tightly to my breast. "Mark, honey, you know you're so special to me. I love you. I think you're such a fine little fellow, and I don't like to see you acting this way." I felt him relax a bit. "You know, Mark, I had a little boy just like you. His name was Greg, but I don't have him anymore. He died." Mark looked up at me now as I talked. "Greg loved Matchbook cars. Do you like those cars?"

He shook his head vigorously up and down.

"I'll tell you what I'm going to do. Tomorrow I'll bring you one of Greg's cars. Would you like that? I know Greg would like you to have one."

Mark nodded yes, then gently relaxed his head on my breast. I felt some of the fight drain out of him. I began to hum and rock. In a while, his body went limp as he fell fast asleep. I cradled him in my arms and wiped the perspiration from his tiny forehead.

Ever so quietly, God crept into my heart and whispered softly, "Becky, you're just like Mark. I've tried to talk with you all these months, but you kicked and screamed so loud you couldn't hear me. It's okay. I know you're hurt. I've just had to hold you tightly until you could calm down. If you'll let me now, I'll cradle you in my arms and you can rest. You can trust Me. I won't let you go."

Emotionally I felt the fight drain out of me. For the first time in nine long months, I no longer had the strength to struggle. If I were to survive any longer, it would have to be with God's strength, not my own.

I looked at little Mark asleep in my arms. Suddenly I knew that just as I loved Mark and wanted what was best for him, God loved me, too. If Mark could trust me to love and protect him, I could trust God even more for His love and protection.

Like a little child, I saw myself crawl into God's arms. I felt them tighten around me and pull me close. I was so weary. Now I could rest in His arms.

CHAPTER FIFTEEN

Christmas for Two

ONE *night, not long after my episode with Mark, Harold Morris called, his voice full of excitement.* "Becky, I've got a special friend who recently moved to Asheville. Her name is Betsy Richardson. She's a godly woman who really loves the Lord. If anybody in this world can help you, she can. You've just got to meet her."

"How am I going to do that? I can't imagine simply showing up at her doorstep and saying, 'Here I am. Harold said you'd help me.' "

"As soon as I can get away, I'll come up and take you," he promised. "You're going to love her. She's married to Bobby Richardson. Do you know who he is?"

"Should I?"

"Becky Smith, I can't believe you," he said, with a hint of disgust in his voice. "Bobby Richardson is only the most famous second baseman the New York Yankees ever had. Don't you keep up with baseball?"

"I'm sorry," I mumbled.

I was soon to discover that God has many ways of working His plan in our lives. Not long after my conversation with Harold, I picked up a Sunday edition of the Asheville paper after church. At home, I changed into a pink jogging suit and stretched out on the living room floor with the paper. The warm afternoon sun, streaming in the window, helped me relax. Tonya and Emily, a neighborhood friend, hurried to the bedroom to play.

As usual, I turned first to the women's section and scanned the new brides for familiar faces. On page five, a woman's picture caught my eye. The name underneath read Betsy Richardson. I bolted upright and quickly scanned the announcement. Betsy Richardson was going to be the featured speaker at the Christian Women's Club in Asheville the following Thursday. I could not believe it. I ran to call Harold.

"Go, Becky! Stay all night if you have to, but don't leave without introducing yourself to Betsy. Make sure she knows you're the one I've been telling her about."

I hung up, then immediately dialed Lula Mae Briggs, my spiritual mom. "Will you go with me Thursday night to hear Betsy Richardson speak in Asheville?" I asked breathlessly.

"Sure, I would love to go. Is she Bobby Richardson's wife?"

"You know Bobby Richardson?"

"Of course! He played baseball with the New York Yankees. Everybody knows who he is."

I chuckled to myself and quickly responded, "I'll pick you up about six."

On Thursday, as Lula Mae and I left for the meeting, she said, "Becky, I've been praying for you. I've asked God to put the right people in your life, friends who will help build and strengthen your faith." Neither of us realized then that God was about to answer her prayer in His own unique way.

The cafeteria meeting room in Asheville was buzzing with activity when we arrived. Finally we located a table with two unclaimed spaces and sat down to wait. A few moments later, I spied Betsy taking her place at the head table. Quickly I excused myself and headed straight for her. "Hello, Betsy," I said hesitantly. "My name is Becky Smith. I'm a friend of Harold Morris."

"Oh, Becky," she said sincerely, her blue eyes shining as she cupped my hand in both of hers. "I'm so happy to meet you. We've all been praying for you."

Immediately I felt a bond of love and trust with her. How could I not love someone who had been praying for me when she did not even know who I was?

"I want you to come visit our home," Betsy continued. "Stay after the program tonight, and we'll work out a time."

"Okay," I agreed, then retreated to my seat as the program began.

When Betsy spoke, her voice was soft and warm. She told us about her early marriage to a professional baseball player, their five children and how the Lord had directed their lives. She talked openly about her relationship with God. Her love for Him was obvious. I was deeply moved by her transparency. After the program, Betsy and I set a time for our first visit. I went home excited, knowing I would get to spend more time with such a special lady.

The week after that, when Tonya and I stepped inside the Richardson home for our visit, we were immediately surrounded by love. Bobby and the children were just as open and warm as Betsy. Three of their children, Christy, Jeannie and Richie, were still at home, and the entire family quickly incorporated us into their lives.

In the following weeks, Tonya and I traveled often to the Richardson home, perched on a mountainside on the grounds of the Ben Lippen

Christian School. Their schedule was filled with activities, but we were always included. I especially enjoyed attending high school games and cheering for Christy and Jeannie, who played on the varsity basketball team. Being involved in their lives gave me back a sense of what I had lost at East High.

Betsy and I often lingered with an open Bible beside a warm fire, drinking hot chocolate, talking and praying. Constantly she reassured me. "Becky, I don't understand why the accident happened any more than you do. But I do know one thing. God is in control. He's real and He loves you. He has a plan for your life, even as a single woman."

The Richardsons were different than any family I had ever known. For a while, I could not quite put my finger on what made them different. Gradually I began to see that it was their relationship with the Lord. They actually treated Jesus as if He were real to them; He was a part of their daily thoughts and conversations. His presence determined how they lived, the kind of music they listened to, even the books they read. God was teaching me about Himself through the lives of His children.

Thanksgiving came and went. I tore November off the calendar and braced for the Christmas season. How I longed to skip over December and move straight into the new year. I knew from experience, however, there was no way to get through it but straight ahead one day at a time, one moment at a time.

Wanting to make Christmas as happy as possible for Tonya, I decided we would do things just as we always had. She needed to know we were still a family, a family of two with traditions to maintain and a heritage to cherish.

The first Sunday afternoon in December, the two of us bundled up and set out in the stinging cold to search for a Christmas tree. After several stops, we finally located our prize at a roadside stand. The man stuffed our six-foot balsam into the trunk of the car and secured the lid with a string. Tonya hopped up in the front seat, sat backwards on her knees and watched the tree bob up and down all the way home. Her happiness warmed me.

The two of us finally managed to drag the huge tree inside and secure it upright in front of the living room window. We then stopped to bake our traditional Christmas cookies. Tonya put "I'm Dreaming of a White Christmas" on the stereo, and we hustled around the kitchen getting the cookie dough ready. Soon the delicious aroma of chocolate chip cookies wafted through the air.

Between bites of warm cookies and cold milk, we wrapped the tree with blinking lights and tied red bows on the branches. We hung paper chains and homemade ornaments Tonya and Greg had created. Every decorated jar lid, bread-dough creation and hand-painted wood ornament carried a special memory.

Our latest additions were delicately blown eggs. Greg had learned to do them in art class. The four of us had spent a happy Sunday afternoon blowing, carving and decorating them with glitter and ribbon. Gently Tonya and I placed each delicate egg on the tree. I saved the best egg for last. Inside, resting on a white cotton cloud, Greg had placed a miniature boy and girl in red stocking caps. They reminded me of Greg and Tonya. Tears puddled my eyes as I hung the ornament in a place of honor, high on the tree. The tiny egg was like life, precious and fragile.

"Okay, T-Bug, it's time for the star," I said, brushing away the tears. "Come on, I'll lift you up." Every year, she would sit on her daddy's shoulders and put the star on top of the tree. She hopped up in a chair and waited for me to pick her up.

"Don't let me fall, Mama," she cautioned.

"Honey, my arms have been strong enough to hold you for a year. I'm not going to fail you now," I promised.

Carefully she placed the star on the top branch, then she jumped from my arms to the floor. We stood back to admire our handiwork. The colored twinkling lights, reflecting in the window, were dazzling. We felt proud of our first Christmas tree as a family of two.

"Daddy and Greg would love it, wouldn't they, Mama?"

"Boy, would they!"

"Do you think they can see it?" she asked.

"Oh, I think so, honey. I think they watch over us all the time, don't you?"

"Wonder what Christmas is like in heaven?" asked Tonya. "I bet the angels are singing and flying around all over the place. Are Daddy and Greg angels now?"

"I don't know, but if they are, they're the best angels up there, right?"

"Yeah. I still miss 'em, Mama, don't you?" she said sadly.

"I sure do. I guess we'll always miss them."

"You know when I miss Daddy the most? When I go to bed. I miss our secret signals when he kissed me good night."

"Well, sugar pie, it's about time for you to hop in bed now. Will you teach me the secret signals?"

"Nope," she said matter-of-factly.

Full of cookies and milk, she fell quickly asleep when I tucked her in bed and played with the curls at the nape of her neck. "Good night, honey. Sweet dreams," I whispered, kissing her lightly on the forehead. "I love you."

As I crawled into bed and turned out the light, memories of our last Christmas as a family tumbled slowly through my mind in the darkness. A little wise man, his headpiece flapping in the wind. An auburn-haired angel with a crooked wing. Mount Olivet Baptist Church. A lonely graveyard in the moonlight. Greg dressed in his new green suit, making faces at himself in the mirror. Tonya, our little princess, decorated with ribbons and lace.

Just one short year ago we were a happy family of four. Now we were two, struggling to feel like a family. Tears fell softly onto my pillow as I slid my hand searchingly across the empty sheet beside me. I ached for Sonny's arms around me.

CHAPTER SIXTEEN

A Mother's Treasures

I could hardly wait for the school holiday break. Tonya and I planned to spend Christmas with Granddaddy and Grandmother Smith. First, however, I had agreed to participate in the annual Christmas musical at church. My choir director asked me to share with my church family what the past year had been like for Tonya and me.

In preparation for that sharing, I meditated deeply about God and His gift to us of His Son, Jesus. I read and reread the Christmas story from the Bible, along with numerous other books on theology.

It seemed incomprehensible to me that God would choose to confine His power into the body of an infant. Why would He allow that child to be born and grow up to be a man, only to die on a cross? How God must have grieved, even as I grieved, to have His Son die. Yet He allowed it so we could know Him. I was awed by that love.

Putting my thoughts and emotions into words and sharing them with the church was a wrenching experience. When the program was finally over, all I felt was tremendous relief. I wondered why I had been willing to put myself through the torture of sharing my pain. Even though I understood more about God, I still did not feel any closer to Him.

Tonya and I left for Florida the next morning. Floy was scheduled to join us, and I was looking forward to our time together.

On Christmas Eve Tonya wanted to spend the night with Kat and Howard, so she could enjoy the excitement of Santa's arrival with baby Amber. Tonya got up early and scrambled out of bed. I watched her eagerly scoop up the goodies Santa left under the tree. I had bought her everything she had asked for and anything else I thought she might enjoy.

When the last package had been opened, she assessed her stockpile. Then with sadness in her eyes, she asked, "Mommie, is that all there is?"

My heart fell. "Yes, honey, that's all there is."

I felt angry with her for wanting more and frustrated with myself for not being able to provide more. Yet I was not capable of giving her what she wanted most—her daddy, her brother and the joy of Christmas like it used to be.

In the following days, Floy and I talked often, comparing notes on how we had survived the previous year. We discovered how different our grief patterns had been.

When Floy returned home after the accident, she had immediately cleaned out Richard's apartment and disposed of his belongings. She had given away Jack's and Richard's clothes and sold their cars within a few weeks. The cars were a daily reminder of her losses, and it was too painful for her.

In contrast, I found comfort in the familiar. Even after a year, Sonny's clothes still hung in the closet and Greg's room was just the same as he had left it. Floy had forced herself to confront and deal with the issues as they arose. I tried to hide and push mine away. Grief, we both discovered, was intensely personal. No two people grieve the same.

Floy told me about a nationwide support group she had attended called Compassionate Friends. Its membership was made up of people who had lost a child. She had found healing in the support of those who understood the kind of pain she was experiencing.

Somehow Floy and I had continued working and had struggled to keep our lives on an even keel. Floy had also experienced a barrage of other life-changing events within a nine-month span. Carol, her youngest daughter, had left for college; and Peggy, her oldest, had married. Floy was now alone. Determined to give Peggy a happy wedding, Floy put aside her pain and helped her daughter shop for the perfect gown and plan a lovely wedding.

"I hurt for Peg," Floy confided. "She missed the thrill of having her daddy give her away or sharing in her happiness."

I cried with her because I realized Tonya, too, would someday face the same experience. Memories of a play wedding in our downstairs den, years earlier, danced through my mind as we talked. Tonya and I were playing tea party one day when she begged me to let her dress up in my wedding gown. I took it out of storage for her. By pinning, tucking and tying, we finally fixed it so she could walk without tripping. By the time her daddy and Greg arrived home from school, she was ready for her big wedding.

While I screeched out "Here Comes the Bride," Sonny proudly escorted her down the steps to the den. When they reached the bottom of the stairs, he dropped to his knees. He looked like a miniature groom, escorting her to the fireplace. Greg and Doodles, our black poodle, were waiting for them. Acting like a clown, Greg married her to an imaginary bridegroom with a wart on his nose.

As Floy and I continued to share our grief, I realized that even though Floy appeared to be so strong, she confessed to as much confusion as I had felt. Neither of us had yet made it through a single day without crying. Life did not make any more sense to her than it did me. Even after a year, we were both still deeply mired in our grief.

Floy confided, "I often find myself saying, if tomorrow is going to be like today, I'm not going to make it." I knew exactly how she felt.

We agreed that grief was indeed a process, seemingly a never-ending one. A flash of memory, a certain song, even the smell of a favorite fragrance could trigger an emotional tornado that could leave us devastated. We wondered if there would ever be an end to it.

I found healing in my time with Floy. Knowing she truly understood and shared my pain, gave me comfort. Renewed in spirit and by our time together, I returned home determined to make changes in my life.

My first project was Greg's room. I knew it was time to begin sorting through his belongings. I waited until a Saturday when Tonya could spend the day with her friend Shannon. I wanted to be alone. Steeling myself for the task, I fixed a cup of coffee and carried it to the bedroom. Locking the door behind me, I surveyed the room one final time. I wanted to remember every detail.

Greg's bulletin board faced the door. Slowly, I began taking down the items—autographed pictures of Meadowlark Lemon and Wilt Chamberlain, a snaggled-tooth self-portrait Greg had drawn in kindergarten, and a newspaper clipping about his first basketball game. His name was circled in red: Smith, 2. Beneath an East High School banner, I found a note he had written to Tonya. Tears sprang to my eyes as I read:

Dear Tonya,

I love you very much. You are sometimes better than having a brother. You are very kind. I hope I am too.

Sometimes I go back and think about our colt. It was a nice colt. I can remember when you were just a baby. You looked cute then. Now your 5 years old sometimes I want you to be a baby again.

Your brother,

Greg S.

Next I sorted through his chest of drawers. Opening the top drawer, I took out his T-league softball shirts, soccer shirts and numbered basketball jerseys. As I folded and boxed his clothes, faces of his friends raced through my mind. I wanted someone to have the shirts who could use them.

When I reached into the bottom drawer and picked up the last shirt, I jerked back in surprise. His ragged Johnny coat was neatly folded on the bottom. Tears sprang to my eyes as I held the size two, red-and-gray-plaid blazer.

Whenever Greg was lonely or needed a playmate, he put on the coat and pretended he was with Johnny, his imaginary friend. Sometimes we pretended Johnny was walking with us to the creek to toss bread crumbs to the fish. Johnny never came to visit, however, unless Greg was wearing the plaid blazer. Greg had played in his Johnny coat until his long arms dangled out of the sleeves. Holding the little blazer, I began to weep uncontrollably.

When I was finally able to stop crying, I opened the next drawer and found the blue-and-white-striped rugby shirt he had worn the day he was elected second vice president of the Student Council at Flat Rock Junior High. I carefully folded his handwritten campaign speech and put it with the shirt. His speech read:

Fellow classmates.

My name is Greg Smith. I am running for 2nd Vice President.

I'm not making any promises to do this or that, but I will try

151

to do my best in office if you elect me as your 2nd vice presi-
dent. I think we're number 1. So I urge you to vote for me.
Thank you.
Greg Smith

I put off the hardest task till last, sorting through the crumpled brown paper bag of belongings they had brought me from the funeral home after the accident. I sat on his bed and held the bag for a long time, trying to bolster my sagging courage and shut out the memories of that awful day.

Finally, turning the bag upside down, I carefully poured the contents onto the bed. My hands trembled as I began sorting through the items. I picked up the watch we had given him for Christmas, just two days before the accident. The time read 2:10 P.M.

Was that the very moment of his death? I wondered. *Could life really be over in a single second, in the twinkling of an eye? Are there moments in time by which we measure all of life?*

Psalm 144:4 is really true, I thought. "For man is but a breath; his days are like a passing shadow (TLB)."

I laid the watch back down and picked up Greg's billfold. In the plastic picture holders, he had a picture of me, his daddy, Tonya, himself and his library card. We had visited Plains, Georgia, President Carter's home-town, and I found Billy Carter's autograph. I could still picture Greg and his daddy clowning behind the podium at the Plains train station, acting presidential while I took their photo.

In another compartment, I discovered his fun fishing license signed by I. Will Sinker and D. Worm. The five-dollar bill Uncle Jack and Aunt Floy had given him for Christmas was tucked in the money pocket. I also found a comb, some change, a big pocket knife, and his new Christmas knife, called The Old-Timer, a knife like Granddad's. As I stared at the assortment of treasures from the pockets of my little son from his last day on earth,

I covered them with my body and cried out in anguish. The agony of grief crept into every nook and cranny of my soul.

When I regained my composure, I resumed my task, determined to finish. I carefully put everything back in the crumpled brown paper bag, then folded it closed. Gently I put the bag in a white cardboard gift box and tenderly covered it with Greg's homemade Valentine's and Mother's Day cards. Closing the lid, I secured it with transparent tape, and on the top I wrote with a red-felt marker: Greg's Treasures.

In my heart I knew, just as surely as I had boxed his physical treasures, that I also had to box and store away some of my own motherhood, that part of me a mother experiences only with her firstborn child.

Into my heart box, I began placing motherhood memories: the excitement of feeling Greg's first fluttering movements as he stirred inside me. The absolute wonder in realizing that somehow I was in partnership with the God of the universe as He created life inside me. The miracle of watching my own body change to accommodate his tiny new life. The awe of watching myself change from a child to a woman. The pain of childbirth, so quickly forgotten when the nurse laid my seven-pound-five-ounce son into my open arms. Strange new feelings had surged through me as I examined his little fingers and counted his toes. The inexpressible pride I felt, watching Sonny tenderly cradle his son for the first time.

The delight of Greg's smile would have to be stored in my heart box. The joy of hearing him call us "Dada" and "Mama" the first time. Greg's first step. First tooth. First haircut. First day of school. First basketball goal. First fish. First love. First day of junior high. It all went by so quickly. Now my firstborn was dead.

Never again, in any place or time, would I be able to hug him, help him with his homework, tell him a story or plan for his future. I would never hold or love Greg's child—my grandchild. Gently, I closed the lid on my heart box and picked up my imaginary red felt-tip marker. On top of the box, I wrote: *Mom's Treasures.* A chapter of my life was over.

When I finished cleaning, I hired a builder to remodel Greg's room into a tiny den. We painted, wallpapered, put down new carpet and installed a freestanding fireplace. I bought a new couch, chair and lamps; but I would not allow myself to hang pictures or memorabilia from the past. This was my starting-all-over retreat.

When the room was finished, for the first time in over a year, Tonya and I went home at night, shut the door and built a fire. From then on, she would do homework, and I would make lesson plans. Other times, we would watch TV. Many nights, after tucking her in bed, I would fall asleep on the couch beside the flickering fire.

For a while I stopped running. The constant, jabbing pain was beginning to ease, but a frightening deadness was taking its place. Depression was creeping quietly into my life.

Meanwhile my friend, Harold Morris, enrolled in Southeastern Bible College and moved to Birmingham, Alabama. Even though we continued to talk on the phone two or three times a week, we didn't get to see each other often.

The winter months of February and March were dark and gray as depression warped my spirit. It was subtle, affecting me physically and emotionally. A deep feeling of gloom enveloped me. There were no mood swings; just a deep, permanent sadness.

Nonetheless, life settled into a predictable routine. During the day I taught school. Three afternoons a week, I waited for Tonya while she practiced basketball or took dancing lessons. On Saturday mornings I cheered from the sidelines while she played basketball on the Dana Wildcats girls' team. Sometimes after the games, we drove to Charlotte to spend the night with my friend, Mona McCrary, and her daughter Christy.

Mona and I had graduated from East High together. While I went to college, she took a job at the local General Electric plant, married and helped put her husband through school. Now she found herself in the middle of a surprise, unwanted divorce. We comforted each other in our pain.

Christy was only a year older than Tonya, so they had fun together eating sundaes at Farrell's Ice Cream Parlor or wobbling around the ice skating rink at Eastland Mall. Mona and I often sat up late into the night, talking about our past and trying to figure out what to do about our future.

One Sunday at Mona's church, her Bible teacher suggested I read C. S. Lewis's book, *A Grief Observed*. I bought it and read it eagerly. C. S. Lewis challenged my thinking. He had written the book following the death of his wife, Joy. Somehow he seemed to put words to my feelings. It was a relief to discover that he had questioned God and struggled, just as I was struggling. Increasingly I felt desperate in my search for a faith I could hang onto.

One day in the middle of March, Ann, my teaching partner, suggested I return to graduate school. "Why don't you take some spring classes with me, Becky?" she coaxed.

The mention of graduate school jarred me. It was as though I had suddenly woken up from a long slumber. I had been halfway through my master's program when the accident occurred, but I had completely forgotten about it. I agreed to go with Ann and register for spring classes. Without realizing it, I also took another tiny step on the road from grief to recovery.

As Easter approached, a deep longing to be near Sonny and Greg grew within me. Visiting their graves was so painful, I had only done it a few times. I asked Dottie if Tonya could spend Saturday night with her, so I could go early Sunday morning and be alone at the graves.

As daybreak spread gently across the morning sky, I wound my way up "Ballard's Mountain" to the little country graveyard beside the church. I parked the car, got out, then reached back across the seat for the pot of white Easter lilies. I straightened the purple bow and started up the hillside.

It was quiet; the air was still. I placed the Easter lilies in the granite urn at the top of their headstones, then proceeded to pick up the dead leaves and broken pieces of wood blown there by the wind. After I cleaned the graves, I knelt between them and ran my fingers along the chiseled words: "Father. Son. They were lovely and pleasant in their lives and in death they were not divided. II Samuel 1:23."

As my tears dropped onto the cold, gray granite, I grieved for their presence. I still longed for their faces, their laughter and the sound of their voices. But I knew that what I wanted most, I could never have, the heartbreakingly commonplace--our old life together.

Not long after my Easter visit to their graves, I woke up one night from another chilling nightmare. I crawled out of bed and stumbled to the den. Moonlight was streaming through the window as I huddled in the corner of the couch. Life was so meaningless and empty. What was the use of going on? Thoughts of suicide began crawling around inside my head once again.

Why don't you just end it all, Becky? an inner voice whispered. *The pain is never going away. Remember the bottle of Valium the doctor in Florida sent? It has been lying in your jewelry box since the accident. It would be so easy. Just take that bottle of pills and drift off to sleep. It would be painless.*

I got up, walked to my bedroom, closed the door and flipped on the light. Opening my jewelry box, I picked up the bottle of Valium. I popped off the lid and poured the pills into the palm of my hand. I felt no fear. *Go ahead, Becky,* the voice whispered again.

I started down the hall to the kitchen for a glass of water. Suddenly something snapped inside me. "What in the world are you doing, woman?" I said aloud. "Are you crazy? What about Tonya? Who would take care of her? Have you completely lost your mind?"

My hands trembled as I poured the pills back into the bottle. I knew I had lost control. I realized I was now actually capable of committing suicide. Suddenly I was very scared—both of myself and for myself.

The next morning I took Tonya to school and went straight to the doctor's office, where I asked the receptionist to work me in. After completing his examination and hearing my explanation of what had happened, Dr. Culbreth said, "Mrs. Smith, you are severely depressed. Without being too technical, I can tell you there are transmitters in the brain called amines. During depression, actual biochemical changes involving these amines take place. There is medication that can help. It will make you drowsy, so don't take it when you need to drive."

I had the prescription filled on my way home from school. That afternoon I took my first pill. "Tonya, while you watch TV, I'm going to take a little nap," I said. "Will you wake me up about six so we can eat supper, then go to prayer meeting? Don't leave the house."

"Okay, Mama," she agreed. I took a pill and lay down on the couch while she sat on the floor watching TV. In a flash, I was asleep.

When I awoke, I was startled. Tonya was gone, and the clock read six twenty-five. I jumped up, frantic to find Tonya. She was asleep in her bed. I looked out the bedroom window and realized it was morning. I had slept all night.

"Honey, why didn't you wake me up last night?" I said, shaking Tonya awake.

"I tried, Mama, but you wouldn't wake up. I shook you and shook you, but you would fall back asleep. I thought you were just tired."

"I was, honey," I said, trying to act nonchalant. "I feel better this morning after a good night's rest."

Inside I was shaking. I knew I could never take another one of those pills. It was too dangerous. What if something had happened to Tonya? It was a sobering thought. I knew I would have to dig a little deeper into myself to discover the resources I needed to survive. I would not depend on pills.

CHAPTER SEVENTEEN

Don't Let Me Make a Mess of Things

SHROUDED *in the gloom of depression, I discovered another of life's truths. We have many relationships in life, but none* can compare to that of a husband and wife. I ached for the feel of Sonny's arms around me, for the intimacy of his touch. Harold Morris provided the special presence of male friendship, but it wasn't the same as having a husband. My family and friends were dedicated supporters. They loved, prayed and cared for me; but they could not fill the empty spot in my life. A part of me was missing.

One day I met David, a high school classmate. He had been the star of our basketball team. After we reminisced about high school days, I told him about Sonny and Greg. He told me about his divorce.

"Becky, I'd like to take you out to lunch on Saturday," he said before we parted. "Your daughter is welcome to come along."

I was startled. Go out to lunch with a man? "I don't know," I said.

"Think about it, and I'll call you tomorrow. Is your number in the book?"

I nodded yes and hurried down the street, anxious to collect my thoughts. Would having lunch with him be like having a date?

"Honey," I broached the subject to Tonya, "I met an old high school friend today. He wants us to have lunch with him on Saturday. Would you like to go?"

Suddenly anger glinted in her eyes. She clenched her little fist, drew herself up to full height, stamped her foot and bellowed, "I'm not going, and you're not either!"

I realized a dramatic moment in our relationship had arrived. The issue was not whether to have lunch with David; it was one of control. Who was going to control our relationship, Tonya or me? She was testing me. I had to give her some limits.

"Sweetheart, you don't have to go," I said calmly, "but I am going. David will pick me up at twelve. You can be here to meet him, or I'll take you to Aunt Dot's before he arrives. The choice is yours."

"I want to go to Aunt Dot's," she said petulantly.

David and I had a pleasant lunch on Saturday, but I could hardly wait to get away from him. I was fearful my friends would see me and whisper, "Getting over it so soon? I can't believe she's already dating."

I knew I would never get over losing Sonny and Greg. Like my friend, Otho Tankersley, whose legs had been shot off during World War II, a piece of me was missing. I could walk and talk. I looked normal on the outside, but on the inside an essential part of me was gone. I was no longer whole, and I would never be the same again.

Meanwhile, David continued to call and invite me out. I kept declining and then finally offered him an explanation. "No, David, I can't do it. I'm still a married woman, and married women don't date."

"No, you're wrong, Becky," he pointed out. "You're not a married woman. You're thirty-six years old and single. You have a lot of life ahead of you. It's time for you to start thinking about that."

"I will," I promised, nervously twisting Sonny's wedding band, which I was wearing on my middle finger.

"How about dinner next Saturday night?" David pressed.

How would I act? I thought. *What would I wear? Where do married people go on a date?*

"I'm waiting, Becky."

"Okay," I agreed. "Dinner, Saturday night."

Suddenly I felt the same fear and rush of blood I had experienced as a girl, when I used to jump off the second floor porch of my Granddaddy's house. Would I land safely in the sandpile or on the ground and injure myself?

When I told Harold about the date, he cautioned me. "Be careful, Becky. Don't move too fast. I don't want you to get hurt."

I was ill at ease on my date with David. I felt as if I were betraying Sonny. I realized I wasn't ready to date.

One evening in late April, after a revival service at church, God began to quietly stir in my heart and help me resolve some of the questions that had haunted me the past fifteen months. At home, I sat in my rocking chair by the fire and was starting to read my Bible, when it fell open to: "Now faith is the substance of things hoped for, the evidence of things not seen (Hebrews 11:1, KJV)."

As I reflected on this Scripture, I began to realize I would simply have to trust what I could not see. I could not be certain that there was life after death; no one had ever been to heaven and returned to tell us about it. The Bible was the only record I had that heaven actually existed, and God had not revealed very much about the subject. Reading every book that had ever been written throughout the ages could not answer my questions. No one knew for certain what I was trying to understand about life after death.

What if I came to the end of my life and discovered that neither heaven nor hell exist? But, then, what if they really did? I suddenly realized that I had everything to gain and nothing to lose by simply believing Jesus was who He said He was—the Son of God. If believing would help me make it through the rest of my life and give me peace, then perhaps I should choose to believe.

Weary of the constant inner battle, I finally knelt beside my couch and prayed aloud, "Right now, God, I choose to believe in you and your Word. Will you forgive my unbelief, remove any sin in my life that would separate me from you and cleanse my heart? I want to follow you. Will you help me put my doubts and fears to rest?"

Nothing dramatic happened. I saw no flashes of light nor felt a sense of jubilation. God did not shower me with a great sense of His presence. I simply made a choice to believe in the Bible, Jesus and God. I would no longer allow doubts to torment my spirit. When I arose from my knees, the matter was settled.

One night near the end of school, I answered the phone and a strange male voice said, "Becky, my name is John. You don't know me, but I know you. I've been coming to your church for a while. I know your husband and son were killed about a year-and-a-half ago. It's taken me a long time to get up the nerve to call you. I wondered if I might be able to take you out to dinner."

When he paused to catch his breath, I thought, *A blind date? No way!* "I'm sorry, but I don't think so," I immediately responded.

"What if we go out for a cup of coffee after church Sunday night?" he suggested quickly.

"I'll think about it," I said.

He asked if he could call me back on Thursday. When he did, we had a pleasant conversation, and I agreed to go with him for coffee after the

Sunday night worship service.

John turned out to be a pleasant individual, quite a decent man. I agreed to see him again. We began dating, but my guard was always up. I was keenly aware of my own vulnerability. My emotions were in a constant state of flux. I knew I was not ready to be in a relationship that required any emotional involvement, but I had already discovered that loneliness is a powerful force. I longed for companionship.

Meanwhile, Tonya continued to try to reverse our roles. She tried to become the mother and make me the child. She did not want me out of her sight and certainly did not want me to date. I began to realize that something had to be done to halt her growing feelings of responsibility for and control over me.

Summer was approaching, and I thought about sending Tonya for a week of summer camp. Camp would give her the opportunity to have a good growing experience in a protected environment. It would also give us some breathing room and perhaps put the brakes on her struggle to reverse our roles.

After school was out in June, I took Tonya to camp on the appointed Sunday afternoon. I helped her get settled in the cabin, unpack and meet new friends. Reluctantly I kissed her goodbye. When I drove away we were both crying, but I felt I was doing the right thing. Helping Tonya by letting her hurt seemed like such a contradiction.

It was a hard week. I called camp every day to check on her. They said she cried most of the time, so I had to fight the impulse to drive to camp and bring her home. By the time I picked her up the following Saturday, we had both grown through the separation. We were both a little stronger and more independent of each other.

Another unexpected boost in my effort to break our role reversal struggle came in July. Mona, my high school friend, called from Charlotte and said, "Becky, how would you like to take a trip with me?

I'm responsible for planning a leadership meeting for the company executives, and I want to check out a place in Louisiana. When I get through there, I'm coming back to Atlanta to find a place to live. I've received a promotion and am transferring to the offices there. Are you interested in going?"

"You bet!" I responded enthusiastically.

Mona picked me up the following Sunday. We drove to Atlanta and spent the night at the Hilton, planning to use their shuttle service to the airport the next morning. After breakfast, as we walked back to the hotel, we were horrified to see the shuttle bus pulling away without us. We frantically hopped into Mona's old Ford Pinto and raced down the interstate highway as fast as her car could go. The air conditioning was broken, the windows were down, and our hair blew wildly in the wind.

"Faster, Mona," I urged. "We're going to miss the plane. Drive faster."

"I'm peddling as fast as I can," she laughed as we whizzed by cars in the fast lane, the accelerator pressed to the floor.

Roaring into the airport parking lot just as a shuttle bus started back toward the terminal, we yelled for it to wait. We barely made it in time to board the plane and were in the air before I could even reflect on what I had just done. I was flying in an airplane, something I vowed I would never do again.

When we landed in Baton Rouge, Louisiana, Mona rented a car, and we drove to the resort she was checking out. The motel gave us a free room and a guided tour through the facilities. After we returned to the room, Mona flopped on the bed and groaned, "Becky, I just can't bring the folks from my company here. They're accustomed to much nicer meeting places with lots of recreational facilities. This is my first attempt at booking one of our meetings, and now I've made a mess. What in the world am I going to do?"

"Well, let's get a map and see what else is within driving distance," I suggested. We secured a map and began to scan the area. "Natchez, Mississippi, isn't far away," I said. "How about that? I know it's an historical place. But it's getting late, so we'll have to hurry."

We thanked our host and headed for Mississippi. We arrived in Natchez about eleven and headed straight to the Holiday Inn. The gas tank registered empty. I was tired, hungry and had a headache. Mona went inside to get a room but came back looking grim. "They don't have any rooms. The Mississippi Baptist Convention is meeting here, and there are no rooms available in this whole town!"

"Did you tell them we're two single women alone and we absolutely have to have some place to stay?" I practically shouted.

"Why don't you tell them, smartie?" she responded.

"I will," I said, locking the door and slamming it behind me. Mona followed me inside.

"Can you help us find a room?" I pleaded with the desk clerk. "We're two single women traveling alone. We're tired and hungry, and our car is out of gas. Is there any place at all you could think of that might have a room?"

"There is one place," she said. "They do take guests sometimes. Let me call."

Mona and I could tell from her end of the conversation that we were in luck. "Here are the directions," the clerk said, handing us a map. "It's an old historic mansion called The Burn. You'll love spending the night there."

"Oh, thank you, a thousand times thank you," I said as we left.

"Open the door," Mona said when we got to the car.

"I don't have the keys."

"Well, I certainly don't," she hissed through gritted teeth.

We looked inside the car; the keys were hanging from the ignition.

"What now?" Mona said sarcastically. "You've locked them up."

"I'll see if the clerk has a coat hanger. I've never unlocked a car this way, but I suppose it can be done," I said meekly.

For thirty minutes we jiggled the wire coat hanger, trying to hook the door lock. With each passing minute, our nerves and patience with each other grew shorter. By the time we unlocked the door, we were hardly speaking and drove in silence to The Burn.

Even in the dark, we could see the splendor of the old majestic southern mansion as we wound our way up the tree-lined, circular driveway. A hoop-skirted southern belle in her nightcap greeted us at the door and showed us to our private room out back in renovated slave quarters. It was quaint and lovely.

"Please join us in the morning for breakfast. We serve family style in the dining room at eight o'clock," she said, gently closing the door.

Mona and I went to sleep in stony silence. But after a good night's rest, we laughed the next morning about our adventure. I apologized for locking the keys in the car and asked Mona to forgive me. She giggled and said she would think about it.

In the light of day, The Burn was even lovelier than we anticipated. It was a perfect location for Mona's convention. We made all the arrangements, then flew to Atlanta.

After finding Mona an apartment, we left Atlanta and headed back to North Carolina. On the way home, I finally acknowledged a secret I had been carrying inside for some time. I had neither the energy nor the desire to teach school another year. I was simply not willing to force myself into carrying that fragile responsibility any longer. I desperately needed time to take care of myself and heal. The trip with Mona made that clear to me. Even though it seemed like a big financial risk, I felt I could survive for a year on Sonny's employee-death benefits and the small insurance policy. I decided to ask for a temporary leave of absence from my job.

Scheduling an appointment with Mr. Rogers, my principal, I explained my feelings. "Please," I begged him, "I just need some more time away from the responsibilities."

"Let's clear it with Mr. Marlowe, the superintendent," he suggested. "It's fine with me if he approves."

"Take all the time you need," Mr. Marlowe said when I asked him about it. "Your job will be waiting when you're ready to return."

I was grateful. For the first time in my life, I felt a great sense of freedom. I had gone from high school into college, then straight into teaching; from marriage into motherhood, then returning to the routine of teaching. There had never been a time in my adult life when I did not have the responsibility of someone else's life or schedule. Now I was responsible only for myself and Tonya.

One night Lula Mae, my spiritual mom, invited me to a makeup party with six other women. We sat around the table, took off all our makeup and laughed at each other as we learned new techniques of applying eyeliner, eye shadow and blush. One lady, Lora Lohman, was the life of the party. She joked about her chubby cheeks and kept us all laughing with her sharp wit. It felt good to laugh. For me, it was a sign that the pain was starting to ease, and I was beginning to heal.

Lora called the next day and invited me to the September Christian Women's Club luncheon. The speaker was a striking woman who shared her testimony of how God became real in her life through her struggles, following the suicide of her teenage daughter and later the death of her husband from cancer. As she closed, I thanked the Lord for showing me an example of such courage. I asked Him to help me have that kind of relationship with Him.

That afternoon Lora called to tell me about two other events she wanted me to attend. One was a prayer coffee, the other was an eight-week Bible study. My first prayer coffee was an experience much like my first club meeting. I was amazed to hear women openly sharing hurts, disappointments and sorrows. They actually wrote down prayer requests, then broke into small groups to pray for the needs. They prayed for me, calling my name and asking God to heal my hurt and show me His plan for my life and for Tonya's. I felt completely surrounded by their love.

Bible study was the same. Eight women met once a week to pray and study the Bible together in a home. We were given a study guide and a Bible. I was relieved to find that the study book referred to the Bible passages not only by name but also by page number. I could flip to the correct page and find the passage without being embarrassed.

I also discovered how little I knew about the Bible, but I was determined to learn. I asked the Lord to give me a heartfelt hunger for Himself and to teach me His ways. I tried diligently to study every day and spend time in prayer. If my mind began to wander, I would stop and ask Him to refocus my attention.

I began to realize that to know God personally, I needed to study His Word daily. Reading the Bible was a real act of coming into His presence. If I did not spend time in His Word, I would never get to know Him.

I found a powerful truth for my life in 2 Samuel 14:14, "All of us must die eventually; our lives are like water that is poured out on the ground—it can't be gathered up again (TLB)."

I did not want to waste my life like water running down a drain. Certainly Sonny's and Greg's deaths made me realize just how temporary life was. I felt a growing sense of urgency to find God's will for myself as a single woman. Would He show me the way? I wanted to believe He would.

Soon life settled into a predictable routine of taking Tonya to and from school each day, Christian Women's Club meetings, Bible study, prayer coffee, church and choir rehearsal. I was also serving as district director for the Business and Professional Women's Clubs and was responsible for ten clubs in the western North Carolina mountain region. I had much to keep me challenged and occupied.

On a deeper level, I also began to understand that God did not cause the airplane to crash and kill Sonny, Greg, Jack and Richard. When He created the universe, He established laws from which it would operate. He chooses not to tamper with them. One of those was the law of gravity. When an airplane flies too low, the force of gravity causes it to crash.

When a loved one dies of cancer, it is not because God inflicts the disease on him or her. Rather, disease is a product of man's original sin.

Disease is no respecter of persons, nor does God choose its victims. Finally understanding these truths helped soften my heart toward God. I no longer held Him responsible for the pain in my life.

As I continued to grow spiritually, I felt my life coming back into focus. A portion of another verse became my daily prayer, "Lord, don't let me make a mess of things (Psalm 119:31b, TLB)."

CHAPTER EIGHTEEN

Tonya's Delayed Reaction

*C*AUGHT *up with my new friends and growing spiritual adventure, Christmas arrived before I knew it. Tonya and I* decorated for Christmas again. Then we headed for Florida when school was out for the holidays.

A second year had passed since the accident. The emotional roller coaster I had been riding had slowed, and my life had begun to level out. The future still carried a big question mark, but I was grateful some of the pain had eased.

Granddaddy and Grandmother Smith seemed stronger, too. It was good just to be near them. Once again, their love soothed the tender places in our lives.

The night before Tonya and I were to return home, she woke me up, thrashing and groaning. Flipping on the bedside lamp, I shook her awake. "Honey, are you dreaming?"

Startled, she sat up and rubbed her eyes."Oh, Mama, it was awful," she said, gently stroking my face.

"Do you want to tell me about it?" I asked.

"No, I don't want to talk about it."

"Then lie back down. Everything will be all right," I said softly, stroking her forehead until she went to sleep again.

We left early the next morning. Tonya was strangely quiet all day. Late in the afternoon, she began to cry. "Mama, last night after we went to bed, you fell asleep and I was still awake. You lay so still, I couldn't tell if you were breathing. I thought you had died, too. I was so scared. What would happen to me if you died? I wouldn't have anybody in the world to take care of me," she said with a sob.

I pulled her to me. "Nothing's going to happen to me."

"You don't know that."

"You're right, I don't," I said. "Let's talk about it." After we decided who could take care of her if anything happened to me, Tonya asked, "Can I ask Og and Lib Freeman to be my godparents? I know they love me."

"Sure you can, honey. I think they might love that."

At home, Tonya became increasingly fearful. When she spent the night with Crysti, Tiffi or Shannon, she would sometimes call me at two or three o'clock in the morning to come get her. It was scary.

I watched her intently; she seemed distracted and withdrawn. At night she cried and did not want to go to sleep. Then she woke up crying because of bad dreams. Finally I did something I vowed I would never do: I let her sleep in my bed. She seemed to feel safe close to me.

One day school was out due to a heavy snowstorm. Emily, a neighbor friend, invited Tonya outside to build a snowman. It was the first time since the accident that she had ventured out to play in the snow. When they finished playing, Tonya came inside and hopped into a bathtub of warm water. As I walked by the bathroom door, I heard her talking aloud.

"Daddy, we all had fun in the snow today, didn't we?" she said. "Boy, we got old Greg good one time. I really miss you. Does it ever snow where you are?"

Oh, my God, I thought, desperation surging over me. *My baby's in trouble.*

That night she had the worst nightmare of all. She awoke screaming, then suddenly started laughing.

"What's wrong, honey?" I asked.

"Mama, Daddy and Greg are all right. They didn't die after all. They weren't in those caskets. Somebody else was. They were here yesterday and played in the snow with me. They came back tonight. I talked with them."

"What did they say?" I asked, trying to sound casual.

"They came to see me at school. I walked into my classroom, and they were waiting for me. Greg has grown up now, Mama. He's got his driver's license. He's been driving Daddy around in a van. Daddy's in a wheelchair. Greg isn't hurt, but Daddy's pretty crippled. When I saw them, I ran to give Daddy a hug but he said, 'Don't touch me.' "

"Oh, honey," I injected, "you know Daddy would never tell you that."

"Mama, he was hurt!" she screamed. Her little face was contorted with pain; anger danced in her eyes. The nightmare had been real to her.

"How did they look?" I asked, trying to calm her.

"Just wonderful. They said they still loved us. For a while they lived in a motel, till they bought the van. They're coming back, Mama, they promised."

Holding her close, I anxiously wondered how to help her. I could not make the nightmares go away. I realized Tonya and I both had missed an important point of closure when Sonny and Greg died. We never saw their bodies. I had even caught myself fantasizing that they might come walking back into our lives. I was not surprised that she had done the same.

Nonetheless, two years had passed. Why was she having this reaction now? Perhaps she had matured to the point that she could grasp the finality of death. Now she understood that they were really never coming back.

On our way to school the next morning, Tonya was unusually subdued. She asked, "Mama, will you walk me to my classroom today?"

"Sure, honey," I agreed.

As we walked into the building, she held my hand tightly. When we neared the classroom door, she became fearful.

"You go first," she said when I started to push the door open.

Still holding her hand, we stepped inside the classroom. Diane and Mary were standing around the aquarium. "Hey, here's Tonya," Diane said, running to meet her.

When her friend greeted her, Tonya finally relaxed. The dream had been so real, she was afraid of what she might find in the room.

At home, I called my neighbor, Ron Metzger. He was director of Hendersonville's Mental Heath Clinic.

"Ron, I've got to have some help. Tonya is having some strange reactions lately," I said, telling him the story. At the close of our conversation, Ron promised to get right back to me as soon as he could make the arrangements for some counseling. A short while later he called to tell me we had an appointment with Dr. George Beckwith, the child psychiatrist on their staff.

Our first appointment was on a wet, silvery day in February. I took a cross-stitch project to keep my hands busy. Tonya appeared at ease and not at all anxious. We were escorted to a tiny room and greeted by Molly, a counselor who said she would be working with us after our sessions with Dr. Beckwith.

After our interview with Molly, a distinguished, middle-aged man with salt-and-pepper hair and black horn-rimmed glasses entered the room.

"I'm Dr. Beckwith," he said, shaking my hand and Tonya's. Looking directly at me, he said, "Mrs. Smith, we're here today for Tonya. It will be necessary for her to answer our questions and talk with us. We want you to allow her to do this. Don't answer for her."

I felt as if I had been reprimanded. "Yes sir," I said, taking out my cross-stitch hoop.

"Tonya, I understand you've been having some bad dreams. Why do you think that's happening?" he asked, sternly staring directly into her eyes. His countenance was cold, demanding. Tonya began to squirm as Dr. Beckwith waited in silence for her response. The wait was uncomfortable, unnerving.

Tonya looked at me, her eyes pleading and filling with tears. I could see them saying, *Please help me, Mommie.*

I fought the urge to gather her in my arms and walk out. Instead I quickly glanced away and pretended to be absorbed in my needlework.

The doctor waited. The silence continued. Finally Tonya said quietly, "I don't know. I guess it has to come out somehow."

"Tell me about your dreams, Tonya," he continued. Again, he waited.

Finally she began, "One time I was in my room and heard little rocks hitting my window. Daddy and Greg were calling, 'T-Bug, psst. T-Bug. We're down here.' I went to my bedroom window, and they were on the ground. They told me they were okay."

As she continued to spill out her nightmares, I cried inside. My heart was breaking for my baby.

When Dr. Beckwith started to wrap up our session, he said, "Tonya, I think your first response to me was correct. Your grief had to come out some way, and it's coming out in your dreams. We're going to try to help you. I want you to come back and see Molly. She will have some things for you to do, and it will be necessary for you to talk with her. Things are going to get better for you, Tonya, I promise."

When he left the room, Tonya ran to me, and I hugged her close. I could not stand to see her hurt, yet I knew no other way to help her. I had done my best, but I did not know how to take away her pain. We would just have to work through it together.

For the next three appointments, I was not allowed in the room with Tonya. She spent the time alone with Molly. Afterwards, I studied Tonya's facial expressions and watched her for any sign of agitation or fear. I questioned her carefully about their discussions. She seemed to be talking freely with Molly about Sonny and Greg and about her recollections of home and family. She seemed totally relaxed each time, not at all stressed.

At the end of her third visit, Molly suggested I come alone the next time. I was anxious to hear her comments.

She said, "Mrs. Smith, first of all, I want you to know that you've got a healthy, happy child. I'm amazed she has been able to cope as well as she has. I don't see any signs of maladjustment or deep residual unresolved grief. I think perhaps Tonya's first response to Dr. Beckwith was correct. Her grief is simply coming out in the form of nightmares. Let me share some of the methods I've used to find out what Tonya's thinking and feeling.

"Oftentimes," she explained, "a child can draw his or her feelings easier than explaining them. I asked Tonya to draw me a picture of her home and family. This is what she did," Molly said, showing me a drawing.

I examined the picture carefully. It was a detailed likeness of our home. The curtains were open, and through the picture windows you could see our couches, coffee table and chairs. Red flowers were blooming in the flower box. Standing on the lawn, side by side, were striking likenesses of Sonny, Greg, Tonya and me. The picture had a warm feeling about it.

"Next," Molly continued, "I asked Tonya what her happiest memories of childhood were. What do you think she said, Mrs. Smith?"

Thoughts of special times raced through my head—our trip to Washington, D.C., or to Canada. Our vacation at Disney World and Six Flags or our camping trips to Myrtle Beach. I shook my head, puzzled.

"Tonya said the happiest memories of her childhood were the times you, her daddy and brother walked in the woods on Sunday afternoon. She told me about the hideout she and Greg had and about the path to the stream where you picnicked and played in the water. Isn't it something, it's the simple things she treasures most? You and Mr. Smith must have been wonderful parents. Tonya certainly seems to have absorbed some strong, important values. She's a healthy child. You've done a good job helping her work through the grief process."

I started to cry. It was the first time someone had ever validated me as a single parent. It had been a heavy load, and I sometimes felt like a failure. I was often so absorbed in my own grief and fighting for my own emotional survival, I was not sure I was aware enough of Tonya's needs. I felt a terrible burden of guilt, because I could not be all she needed or wanted. I could not give back to her what had been taken away, and I felt inadequate to make up the loss to her.

Molly handed me a box of facial tissues and patted me on the hand. "You don't want to be here, do you, Mrs. Smith?"

"No," I sobbed, "I thought Tonya and I were handling things pretty well alone. I've done all I know to do."

"It's okay to admit you need help," Molly continued. "Let me tell you a story. You know, a farmer can plow a field with a horse and an old-fashioned plow. He can do a good job, too, getting the rows fairly straight and planting a crop that flourishes. Another farmer might use a tractor to plow his field. He can do just as good a job as the farmer with the horse and plow, but he can do it faster. His crop can be just as bountiful as the first farmer's.

"You can handle your grief and Tonya's, but perhaps we've got some methods and suggestions which can help you do the job a little faster, a little more thoroughly. It's no disgrace to ask for help when you need it. I believe you've done right in seeking help for Tonya. She's not going to require any more visits. But I want you to call us if you need us. We're here for you."

I thanked her and left. On the way home, I prayed, "Thank You, God, for directing me here. Thank You for Ron Metzger, Dr. Beckwith and Molly. Thank You for their knowledge and skill, but most of all, thank You for Your presence in my life. Please help me continue to trust You."

CHAPTER NINETEEN

Through the Valley

ONE weekend in early April, Cheryl and Skip, my niece and her husband, invited Tonya and me to visit them in Atlanta the following weekend. They had bought their first new home and had joined a vibrant, new church. They were anxious to show us both of them.

Friday after school, Tonya and I drove to Atlanta. We had fun taking a grand tour of their spacious country home. On Saturday, Cheryl, Tonya and I spent the day shopping at Lenox Square.

When we woke up Sunday morning, a drizzling rain was falling. Surprisingly, my spirits were about as gray as the overcast sky by the time we arrived at the church.

The parking lot was as crowded as a shopping mall at Christmas. The people hurried through the rain, carrying colorful umbrellas that bobbed up and down. Inside, an usher with a red carnation in his lapel directed us to the balcony. I followed Skip, Cheryl and Tonya up the carpeted steps and down an aisle into a pew. Music from a majestic pipe organ filled the air. An atmosphere of expectancy and excitement prevailed.

Hanging from the ceiling, in the center of the auditorium, was a magnificent crystal chandelier. Hundreds of tear-shaped crystal droplets shimmered like diamonds, reminding me of the ocean at Myrtle Beach during sunset.

As the service began, the congregational hymns were spirited. I sensed joy among the people. After the choir sang, Dr. William Thomason took his place behind the pulpit.

"This morning," he began almost apologetically, "I feel led to speak on the Twenty-third Psalm. What new can be said of this psalm? It has been the topic of hundreds of books and thousands of sermons, but today I feel the Lord is leading me to speak on it once again."

As Dr. Thomason began to expound on the text, I started to tune him out. I had already memorized the Twenty-third Psalm during my search for answers. I did not know how he could add to my understanding of the passage. I picked up the hymn book and flipped listlessly through the pages. Putting it down, I studied the crystal droplets on the chandelier. *If only I could capture some of that sparkle in my life again,* I thought despairingly.

I felt restless as my mind jumped aimlessly from one thought to another. Suddenly a voice sounding like an echo penetrated my thoughts. " 'Yea, though I walk through the valley of the shadow of death,' " Dr. Thomason quoted. "Folks, God did not say we would walk into the valley and stop. He promised we would walk through it."

A mental picture of Sonny and Greg suddenly flashed before my eyes. They were strolling hand in hand through a lush green meadow. Sonny had his fishing pole on his left shoulder; Greg's was on his right. Sonny was holding Greg's hand, and they were whistling as they sauntered through the valley of the shadow of death.

Very quietly, an inner voice seemed to whisper, "Becky, my child. It's okay. Sonny and Greg are with me."

Like fireworks on the Fourth of July, an explosion burst forth inside me. That was it! Sonny and Greg did not walk into the valley of death and stop. They walked through it. They were alive! In that moment, I knew they were alive.

Silently tears poured down my cheeks as the realization took root in my heart. For the first time since Sonny and Greg had died, I cried tears of joy.

Once again, in His own quiet way and in His own time, God surprised me with the last piece of the puzzle I had struggled for two-and-a-half years to find. *Death is not the end. We merely walk through the valley.*

"Oh, God, my heavenly Father. Thank You, thank You for this understanding and assurance," I whispered silently.

For the rest of the service, I was lost in thought, pulling together all the threads I had gathered on my long spiritual journey. Now I understood with my heart what I had long known with my head. In one final, glorious act, Jesus conquered death for us all. Neither death nor the grave could keep us where we did not belong. The reality of what Jesus did for Sonny and Greg on the cross pierced my heart so deeply, I knew nothing could ever again shake it loose.

In a single, sacred moment on a gray, wet day in Atlanta, Georgia, God whispered to me, His child, "Becky, I gave my Son so that your son might live."

Eternity would not be long enough to praise Him.

CHAPTER TWENTY

What Makes Life Worth Living?

AS the end of school neared, so did my nine months of freedom. I was nearing completion of my graduate degree, and I knew it was time to make a decision about my future. More and more, I sought God's direction for my life. Would I return to teaching at Dana Elementary, or should I move away and start all over again in a new place? Mona and Christy were making a new life in Atlanta; perhaps Tonya and I could, too.

Exams were scheduled for early May. On the night of my final in psychology, I took my time answering the questions, handed in the exam and walked slowly down the winding staircase.

Like a washing machine on the spin cycle, my emotions whirled wildly round and round. I wanted to laugh and cry at the same time. One second I felt proud; the next, incredibly empty. I had just reached one of my major life's goals, but the one person who would have cared the most was now missing. Sonny would have swooped me up in his arms and kissed me. We might have even done a little joy dance.

Sonny always told me he was so proud of me, he wanted to put me up on a pedestal and shout, "Hey, world, look! This is my wife."

Tonight I longed to have him do just that.

As I reached the bottom step, a lady I did not know walked by. I looked at her, shrugged, and said, "I'm finished. I really did it."

She smiled and said, "I'm glad."

In the parking lot I found my car, unlocked the door and got in. I buckled my seat belt and started to back out. Suddenly tears flooded my eyes. Laying my head on the steering wheel, I sobbed from the emptiness and loneliness. Would there ever be a time when I stopped crying for Sonny and Greg? Would the ache ever heal?

Graduation was Sunday, May 11, in the Western Carolina University stadium. My parents along with Mona, Christy and Tonya attended the ceremonies. While they made their way to the stands, I found my place among the graduates assembling across the football field.

When the band started to play, the long line of graduates marched in front of the stadium. As I passed Section C, Tonya was leaning over the rail. I walked by and reached up to touch her outstretched hand. "I love you, Mommy," she said. "I'm proud of you."

"I love you, too," I mouthed and blinked away the tears.

As the commencement speaker began, I found my mind drifting back to an earlier graduation—Sonny's and mine from Berry College. It seemed only yesterday that we had started our life together. We had so many dreams and saw some of them come true. I was grateful for those good years together.

Finally it was time for the diplomas to be awarded. My row started to move down the steps and across the field. As we inched along, I heard someone whisper, "Psst, Mrs. Smith."

The university band was seated nearby, but I did not see anyone I recognized. "Mrs. Smith," someone called my name again. I finally saw Bill Johnston, one of Sonny's former band captains, waving at me. I smiled and waved back. Bill had been such a special young man to us. His dad was the Methodist minister who had helped with Sonny and Greg's funeral.

I heard the announcer call my name, "Rebecca Ballard Smith, Master of Arts in Education."

As I started across the stage to receive my diploma, an explosion of whistling and cheers erupted from the band section. My heart pounded. For the brief moment it took the university president to hand me a diploma and shake my hand, Bill and his band became Sonny's arms around me. That special moment reminded me of the valentine roses Raymond and Clifford had sent me two years earlier. Certainly God had a way of providing little surprises.

On my way home from the graduation ceremonies, I dropped Tonya off to play with her friend Shannon and drove on alone. As my car wheels clicked along the Mills River Highway, my mind began to rummage through events of the past two-and-a-half years. I had come a long way since the accident. I had learned a lot about life and loving, death and dying, grief and living. I had grown in ways I never dreamed possible.

"Becky, would you do it all over again?" I asked myself aloud. "Would you choose to marry Sonny and bear his son, knowing you would have to walk alone through this nightmare of grief? Would thirteen years of love and happiness be worth the price of this pain? "Yes, of course I would," I answered myself. "Without a moment's hesitation. I would go back and do it all over again exactly the same way. I have no regrets."

Suddenly, as if materializing from a soft, white cloud, Sonny's and

185

Greg's smiling faces appeared on the windshield. They were as clear and perfect as they were the day we kissed goodbye. I could see the twinkle in Sonny's eyes and the copper-colored freckles on the bridge of Greg's nose. For a brief moment, I was warmed by their presence. Then, like snowflakes melting in the sunshine, they disappeared.

"Goodbye, my loves," I whispered as their images faded from sight.

In that fleeting moment, I realized that my long battle with grief was being won. My love for Sonny and Greg had not died when they died; it had sustained me through the long grieving process. Now their presence was fading from me. I realized I could no longer hold onto what I could not keep. I had to let them go. I was moved to tears by the tenderness of the moment.

At home, I put on my blue jeans and stretched out on the couch with the Sunday paper. It felt good to be alone and free from pressure.

An article on the editorial page caught my eye. It was titled, "What Makes Life Worth Living?" I put down the paper and stared out of the window at the woods across the road, lost in thought.

What does make life worth living for me? A little auburn-haired girl's laughter. A good night whisper, "I love you, Mommie." A late night phone call from my friend Harold who says, "How have you been today? I care about you." A handwritten love note saying, "I prayed for you today." A pot roast. A valentine rose. The hand of a friend who loves me enough to share the silence and does not need an explanation when I show up unexpectedly at her doorstep. The joy of knowing I have been loved by a wonderful man. A mother's memories of her son tucked away in a little box inside her heart. The steadfast love of good parents and family. The supporting embrace of friends. An unshakable faith in God, born from the depths of despair.

Suddenly brought back to the present by a passing car, I sat upright. The woods across the road came into focus. They were lush and green with springtime, perfect for building a playhouse. I got up from the couch and walked across the road. Pushing back the gray branches full of budding green leaves, I entered the woods and picked my way through the underbrush to Greg and Tonya's clubhouse. Surrounded by sweet memories of their play, I inhaled the woodsy smell. I had loved that fragrance from the time I was a little girl building playhouses on Mount Olivet.

How simple life had been in those make-believe days of childhood when I was Princess Rose. I could pretend and make anything happen in my mind. I could dream dreams and make them come true.

Was the little girl in me still alive? Perhaps a little older, a great deal wiser? Could she dream again? Did I have enough energy and creativity to start all over and build a new life for Tonya and me?

"Sure you can, Rose," a little voice inside me whispered. "With God's help, you can do anything you want to, be anything you want to. You just have to try. Don't be afraid to dream."

Picking my way through the briars, I started to shuffle through the dead leaves, hunting for our path to the creek hidden deep in the woods. Suddenly, there it was. Nestled safely in the shadow of a giant oak tree, I saw God's sign of hope for new life in the spring.

A delicate pink lady slipper was beginning to bloom.

Epilogue

THANK *you for sharing my life through the pages of* Keepsakes for the Heart. *After I found the lady slippers in bloom, I spent* a week with Mona checking out the job market in Atlanta. But then I cried for two weeks when I returned home. Uprooting, moving and starting over in a strange place simply seemed too overwhelming.

In July, Tonya and I flew to Houston. Her dance troupe participated in and won the National Junior Tap Championship. Afterwards we spent some time with Floy's family in Arlington.

Returning home in August, I was surprised to discover that Dr. Dean Weaver had accepted a new pastorate in South Carolina. Since his wife, Jeanitha, had served as our church secretary, the deacons asked me if I would manage the office while they searched for a replacement. Looking back, I believe it was God's way of keeping me still while He worked His plan in my life.

Five months later, on Saturday, January 3 at eleven-ten in the evening, God set His plan in motion with a phone call from Jeanitha Weaver. She asked me to join them for dinner the following Monday night at Morrison's Cafeteria in Greenville, South Carolina.

We set the time for seven and just as we were hanging up, she added, "Becky, we've got someone we want you to meet. His name is Max Greer. He'll be there, too."

I was nervous as I drove to Greenville, arriving at Morrison's about five minutes till seven. As Max and I were introduced, I quickly registered first impressions. He was about five feet, ten inches, had strawberry-blond hair, blue-green eyes and wore stylish wire-rimmed glasses. He was handsomely dressed in a camel sport coat, navy pants, blue shirt and coordinating tie.

Over the meal, I learned that Max was a forty-one-year-old widower and son of a Baptist minister. He had been married for twenty years to Marion Hester, the daughter of a Baptist minister. They had two children, Melodie, eighteen; and Danny, sixteen. Marion had died following a painful eleven-month struggle with cancer.

Max's deep commitment to God, his solid inner strength and love for his family was immediately evident. I quickly saw much to respect and admire in him. In addition to his position as Corporate Health and Safety Director of Reeves Brothers, Inc., I also learned that Max served as part-time minister of music at a church. Music—can you believe that?

When Max called the next night and asked me out, I was delighted. Not only did we begin to date frequently, our telephone bills skyrocketed. Sometimes we talked three or four times a day. Before long, we both felt God had opened our hearts and gently placed inside a beautiful, deep love for each other. It took us both by surprise.

On June 6, the day after school was out, Max and I were married in a beautiful church wedding with our children as attendants. Dr. Dean

Weaver and Max's dad, Dr. Daniel Greer, performed the candlelight ceremony that Max and I had written. Melodie and Tonya wore rings made from their father's original wedding bands. Danny wore one designed from his mother's high school ring.

We lit candles in honor and in memory of our lost loved ones: Max's wife, Marion Hester Greer; Sonny, Marion Oliver Smith; and Greg, Marion Gregory Smith. It amazed us that all three of them had been named Marion. Tonya sang "Jesus, We Just Want to Thank You." We all knelt at the altar and wept as Max dedicated our new family to the Lord.

Max and I have been married for nine years now. Every day we are grateful to God for giving us a second chance at happiness with each other. Our love is deep and genuine. We've discovered second marriages are not second-rate. They're different from first ones in many respects, but we've found that our love is no less wonderful. We talk often about Marion, Sonny and Greg. We have never tried to bury the past, but we don't cling to it. We have chosen, instead, to cherish it. The memories bring us joy.

Over the years, we've learned a lot about each other and about blending families. We've been through good times and tough times and have all experienced continual adjustments, especially the children. God has been faithful, however, to meet our every need as He has bonded our hearts and lives together over time.

One of the things I am constantly thankful for is Max's relationship with Tonya. In the beginning, I often pictured them standing on opposite sides of a balance scale. On one side, Max was reaching out to Tonya, offering her the guidance, security and love only a father can give. Tonya, standing on the other side of the scale, could either accept or reject it. I am so grateful that she accepted his love. She has allowed him to become a real father.

When I see the fine young woman Tonya's grown to be, I am reminded of His faithfulness to us during those scary days when I was a single parent. I stumbled often, but I know I did the best I could at the time. I tried never to put our lives on hold as we made a home for two. We planned happy occasions and celebrated small things. I hugged her often and never let a day go by without saying, "I love you."

Somehow God has covered my mistakes with His hand, since Tonya has strong values and a real sense of who she is. I thank Him today for the joy she brings and the beautiful young woman she has become.

Tonya is now a senior at Clemson University, majoring in elementary education. Last year she was the drum major for the Tiger Band. Watching her out front leading that big university band made chills run up my spine, and I had to choke back the tears. Somehow I knew Sonny was punching Greg, saying, "Hey, buddy, look at our little T-Bug."

Max and I now have an empty nest. Melodie and Danny are both married. Melodie earned her degree in nursing and is a successful businesswoman in the medical field. Her husband Craig is studying pediatric cardiology on a medical fellowship. Danny and his wife Tammie were married last year. They live nearby, and he works at the same company where Max is employed.

Today, Floy still lives in Arlington, is active in her church and manages her office for the credit union. She sold the house that Jack and she had built and moved into a garden home. Floy is also a grandmother and especially enjoys her two grandchildren, Leslie and Travis.

Granddaddy and Grandmother Smith remain relatively self-sufficient in Florida. Granddaddy will celebrate his ninetieth birthday and Grandmother her eighty-eighth this year. They have lovingly embraced Max and introduce him as their son-in-law. Their unconditional love continues to amaze me.

As I reflect on my life, I'm astounded at how rapidly the years have flown. And yet it seems only yesterday that I was a little girl pretending to be Princess Rose, spinning dreams of happiness. Now I know that real life is filled with both joy and sorrow.

Twelve years ago after Sonny's and Greg's deaths, the pain in my life seemed almost unbearable and unending. Since then, I have discovered that it was neither. Like a broken bone that needs time to knit back together, my heart has healed over time. Moment by moment, God has given me His strength when I need it.

Even when I felt I had lost Him during the darkest days of my life, He was there. When I ranted, raved and questioned, I found He could handle all my doubts. I've learned to trust Him. He alone knows my future and chooses my path. Nothing touches my life He does not allow.

Furthermore, I have learned to hold life with an open hand. I know that although life is eternal, everything else is temporary. Psalm 146:4 reminds me, "For every man must die. His breathing stops, life ends, and in a moment all he planned for himself is ended (TLB)."

I've experienced the reality of these words as, one by one, my family has diminished in size. After Sonny, Greg, Jack and Richard were killed, my grandparents, Clayton and Estelle Morrow, died. Then my oldest sister Jerlene passed away at the age of forty-four. Two months later, my brother's son Mark, twenty-three, and the only heir to the Fred Ballard name, was killed in a motorcycle accident. My younger sister Margaret contracted polio. My dad survived a stroke, and my mother was recently diagnosed with cancer. We are grateful that radiation therapy seems to have been successful.

Early in our marriage, Max and I asked the Lord to give us a work we could do together. He has given us many opportunities to share through speaking engagements, seminars and a ministry with single adults in our church and community. Because of our experiences, we both feel a great urgency about life and our purpose here on earth. Time is short, and we must tell others about His great love.

Perhaps you have also felt a spiritual need in your own life, as you have read my story. We are all standing on the balance scales of life. Our Lord stands on one side, reaching out to us, wanting to give us the guidance, security and love that only a heavenly Father can give. How it must grieve His heart to have us shut Him out of our lives.

The Lord loves you. He created you, and He died for you. He longs to have you spend eternity with Him. If you do not know Him now as Lord, I pray that today you will invite Him to make a home in your heart. It's really a very simple process. I John 1:9 says, "If we confess our sins, he is faithful and just to forgive us *our* sins, and to cleanse us from all unrighteousness (KJV)."

Prayer is simply talking to God. You could even make this your prayer:

> *Dear Father,*
>
> *I know I am a sinner and need your forgiveness. I believe You died on the cross for me. I now turn from my sins and ask You to forgive me. I invite You to live in my heart and rule my life. I want to follow You. Thank You for saving me. Amen.*

Now that you've opened your heart to the Lord and said this prayer, you need to do the following four things:

First, find a church to attend. Second, seek out someone who really loves the Lord and ask him or her to help you grow spiritually. Third, read your Bible. You cannot ever know Him unless you study His Word. Fourth, talk with the Lord in prayer. Ask Him to help you know and love Him. He will do it, I promise.

Nothing would give me greater joy than to know you have prayed that prayer today and that you've begun your spiritual journey. I hope someday we have the pleasure of meeting in person. If not here on earth, then look for me up in heaven. I'll be there. I pray you will be, too.